ALL CHINA

PASSPORT BOOKS

Trade Imprint of National Textbook Company
Lincolnwood, Illinois U.S.A.

Published by Passport Books in conjunction
with China Guides Series Ltd.

Huang Shan

CONTENTS

ALL CHINA MAP

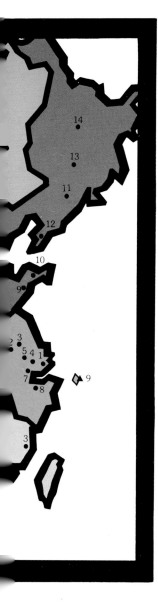

INTRODUCTION:
THE CHINESE KALEIDOSCOPE

China, a civilization of many names and of many guises, has fascinated outsiders over the centuries. They have viewed her with a whole spectrum of feelings from fear to admiration. It has only been in recent years that foreigners have had access to a land that was, for too long, the domain of armchair travellers. Until the 20th century, the exploration of China belonged to intrepid traders and missionaries who often never returned again to their native lands. Yet their tales excited and fired the imaginations of poets, painters and philosophers. And those subsequent interpretations of the tales had an even stronger influence on the west's image of China than the firsthand accounts themselves.

Each of us have the dual image of China and Cathay: a land where heathen savages slaughter innocent missionaries, where proletarian masses chant mindless slogans; and where courtly Mandarins stroll composing poetry by the banks of willow fringed rivers. We are all the victims of conflicting images, which obscure the truth rather than enlighten it.

For the Chinese, since the unification of their land by the Qin Dynasty in 221BC the country has had only one name, the Middle Kingdom, derived from the old belief that China was the centre of the world. All other nations were tributary states which owed allegiance to the emperor, the Son of Heaven. Until the Age of Discovery and Europe's later industrialization, the Chinese had only been in contact with civilizations of lesser sophistication. The first European contact with Chinese civilization was during the Roman era when Chinese-made silk was made available to wealthy Roman matrons through the trading activities of central Asian merchants. There is little evidence, however, that the Romans were aware of the real source of this superb fabric, which aroused opprobrium at the Roman court for being daringly transparent. Nevertheless, it was the Romans who gave the first western name to the Chinese, whom they termed the Seres, the people of silk.

Contemporaneous with the Roman Empire was the rule of the Han Dynasty, which had toppled the short-lived Qin. China during this period was in cultural contact with many of her Asian neighbours, not the least of which was India. This led to the penetration of China by Buddhism, the first and last alien religion to permeate the whole fabric of Chinese life. Buddhism was to influence China's indigenous religions and philosophies, and finally to become absorbed into the pattern of Chinese culture. By the Tang Dynasty, Buddhism was no longer viewed as a foreign religion and its visual representations had lost their Indian influence.

Religion has always been a force for cultural penetration. Before Marco Polo started his epic journey to Cathay, European friars were bringing back to Europe the first accounts of the marvellous Chinese empire. The rise of the Mongol empire in the 13th century had led to the disruption of Moslem rule over central Asia, allowing Christian Europeans to penetrate the central Asian trading routes which, for too long, had been closed by the forces of Islam. In the mid 13th century, the Franciscan friars Giovanni di Piano Carpini and Guillaume de Roubrouck travelled the overland Silk Road as far as Karakorum to bring back reports of China.

However, it was not until the enterprising Polo brothers set out from Venice in 1260 and found their route home from central Asia blocked by war, that European merchants reached as far as the Chinese empire itself. The Polo brothers returned to Europe with the request from Khubilai Khan, the grandson of Genghis Khan, to return to his court with priests. Young Marco Polo accompanied this expedition together with his father and uncle and two friars. The latter never reached Khubilai's court, but Marco survived the journey and was to stay in China for over 20 years.

It is to Marco Polo that we owe our first accounts of the land of Cathay, which have inspired countless painters and poets, including, of course, Coleridge. Marco Polo, while in gaol in Genoa, had dictated them from memory to a troubadour from Pisa called Rustichello. Rustichello embroidered the tales with his own imaginative fancies, and Marco Polo was nicknamed *il milione* for his supposedly untrue million fantasies. Actually Marco Polo is sometimes accurate in his descriptions of China in the 13th century, but Rustichello's stylistic embellishments created a seemingly unreal idea of Cathay, appealing to the poet rather than the historian. In 13th-century Venice nobody could believe that a heathen empire could be even more extensive and prosperous than ancient Rome. Cathay entered into the world of fantasy and fiction. Although China was indeed the most splendid and sophisticated place in the 13th-century world, Europe was not ready to accept such an idea.

In 1601 when the Jesuit Matteo Ricci arrived in Beijing, he was still wondering where he would find the fabulous land of Cathay. It was only after years of living and travelling in China that he came to realise that the Cathay of Marco Polo's accounts had become the China of the Ming Dynasty. The transformation had not taken place in China but rather in Europe. The Renaissance and the Reformation in Europe, and increasing maritime contacts with other parts of the world, had created greater wealth and sophistication in Europe, narrowing the gap between China and the west. However, the gap had not narrowed so much that the Jesuit fathers were not impressed by the splendour and sophistication of the Chinese court, and by the bureaucracy whose efficiency and governmental control was far superior to that under the political systems of Europe, still mainly feudal monarchies. Ricci and the later Jesuits, Schall and Verbiest, urbane and educated though they were, found themselves struggling between contradictory reactions, for their mission of conversion required them to think of the ungodly Chinese as unenlightened and therefore damned.

Jesuit accounts of China — its wealth, social organization and sophistication — created an intellectual stir in post-Reformation Europe. Instead of heightening European perceptions of Chinese civilization, the Jesuit accounts were used as ammunition in a war between the philosophers of the Enlightenment and the Catholic Church. The Jesuits' descriptions of a humane and well-ordered society ruled by a meritocratic system of scholar-bureaucrats appealed to men such as Voltaire. (Ultimately the Jesuit vision of China was influential in the intellectual formulation of the French Revolution.) The Vatican, however, came to the conclusion that the Jesuits were overawed by the sophistication of their potential converts, and unneccessarily accommodating in their adaptation of Christianity to the Chinese way of life. The Jesuits were recalled, disbanded and branded as heretics for their creation of a religion which attempted to blend the tenets of Confucianism with Christianity.

Heavenly Guardian, Huating Temple, Western Hills Park, Kunming

With the withdrawal of the Jesuits from China in the 18th century, the era of intelligent and sensitive observation of China was over. However, the repercussions of such observation had hardly begun. The 18th century saw the cult of *chinoiserie*, which was to stretch over a century and create a more distorted image of China than ever. Europe, hungry for exotic and expensive commodities, increased trade of luxury items along the coasts of China and India. The 18th century brought tea drinking to England. Porcelains, silk and tea were precious, prized goods in Europe.

The European image of China, bearing no resemblance to reality, had an enormous impact on the 18th-century world of letters and fashion. The move away from geometrical to asymmetrical landscaping, which resulted in the fine English country parks of Capability Brown, was based on Jesuit descriptions of Chinese gardens. Yet a cursory look at a Suzhou garden and then a landscaped park in England is enough to show that there is almost no similarity between them. *Chinoiserie* influenced the design patterns of European porcelain, of furniture and even European architecture.

Apart from influencing taste and fashion, the Jesuit accounts of China also had an impact on Europe's political life. The concept of a civil service was introduced, and philosophers debated the values of the Chinese governmental structure to the extent that one English poet, William Whitehead, wrote in 1759:

> Enough of Greece and Rome. The exhausted store
> Of either nation now can charm no more:
> Ev'n adventitious helps in vain we try,
> Our triumphs languish in the public eye....
> On eagle wings the poet of tonight
> Soars for fresh virtues to the source of light,
> To China's eastern realms: and boldly bears
> Confucious' morals to Britannia's ears.

With the industrialization of Europe in the 19th century and the later economic development of North America as a world trading power, the west's vision of China underwent yet another change. The roles began to be reversed. The western trading powers were beginning to gain an economic stranglehold on the world and the system of colonization meant that trade was no longer an exchange of goods between equal partners. The west's rapid industrialization also brought about a sudden transformation in its military capability. Force of arms could be used as a means of creating favourable trading conditions.

The rise of western military power coincided with the decline of the Chinese empire in the 19th century. The west re-evaluated its trading position vis-à-vis China. The latter was no longer seen as a mighty and prosperous empire which could scorn European diplomatic overtures, but rather as a market for Indian-grown opium which could be exchanged for the precious Chinese commodities so desired by the west. British merchants increased the flow of opium into China, and in 1840, when the court commissioner, Lin Zexu, destroyed the imported opium in Guangzhou, the British Parliament decided to go to war to maintain its lucrative trade. The disastrous defeat of the Chinese in the First Opium War made the west realize how weak China's coastal defences were. The Treaty of Nanking in 1842 ushered in the era of the Treaty Ports. From 1842 on, the western powers, and later Japan, competed in establishing economic footholds in the Chinese market.

The Treaty of Nanking destroyed the western image of China as a well-organized state with a benevolent despot and an efficient civil service. China was seen instead as a weak, corrupt state which could be manipulated into signing treaties benefiting western traders. The fabulous vision of Cathay had faded, to be replaced by the image of an entrepreneur's paradise populated by heathen Chinese who sported ridiculous pigtails. Economic and military superiority led to a belief in cultural superiority, fostered by the colonial mentality developed in Africa and India. The 19th century also brought with it a new influx of western missionaries who saw China as an untapped reserve of pagan souls ripe for conversion.

Unlike their Jesuit forerunners, who had arrived on Chinese soil without the backing of military might and faced a society to which they had to adapt, the 19th-century missionaries arrived with gunboats. They had no need to compromise with the existing moral and social codes which they found deeply entrenched within Chinese civilization. This is not to say that the 19th-century missionaries always lacked tact and sensitivity, but there was a prevalent feeling that concessions to missionary activity in the interior of China could be won by force. The Boxer Uprising in 1900, when the peasants of China took up arms against foreign traders and missionaries, can only be understood when one realises that for most Chinese, the missionary had become closely associated with the foreign domination of Chinese soil.

The Boxer Uprising did much to further undermine China's image in the west, and the court's flight in the face of the Allied Expedition on Beijing held the Chinese empire up to world ridicule. The Imperial Palace and Summer Palace were sacked by the allied troops who, in front of Chinese crowds, looted the imperial collection and carried their treasures away as spoils of war.

Chinese intellectuals began to look to the technically advanced west for solutions to their nation's internal weakness. In 1911, when the empire was toppled by a small uprising in Wuhan which quickly enveloped the whole nation, China was left in a political vacuum, searching for a constitutional solution from among western republican models. Jolted into the 20th century by the impact of western trade on her shores, China was now searching for a answer to her problems from the source of her humiliation.

The loss of face was further reinforced in 1918 at the Treaty of Versailles, when China, an ally of Britain and France in the war against Germany, was forced to allow the German concessions on her soil to be handed over to the Japanese rather than be returned to China. This humiliation was too much for the radical Chinese intellectuals of the time. From their protests and demonstrations against the terms of the treaty was born the modern Chinese nationalist movement, ultimately leading to the adoption of Marxism as a practical alternative to western democracy.

From the Republican Revolution of 1911 to the communist takeover in 1949, China's disgrace at the hands of foreign powers was prolonged by the military encroachments of Russian and Japanese troops on Chinese soil, and the western powers' increased economic stranglehold on the treaty ports. Chinese intellectuals developed a strange love-hate relationship with the industrialized west, admiring its political systems, technological superiority and cultural achievements, yet resenting its interference in internal Chinese politics. The invasion of China by the Japanese in 1937, and the backing of the Nationalists by the Americans throughout the Second World War finally led to the alienation of the Chinese intellectuals from the west and their turning instead to the socialist Soviet Union.

In 1949, when Mao Zedong assumed power as the leader of the newly established People's Republic of China, the west stood back in astonishment, amazed that the revolutionary leader and his comrades had wrested power from the American-backed Nationalist government. One explanation the communists give for their victory is based on the popular disenchantment with the Nationalists' war policy. The Chinese people felt the Nationalists were fighting the Japanese only half-heartedly, waiting for the Allied Powers to win for them. Seeing the communists' adamant anti-Japanese stand, as well as their land reform policies, the people gradually transferred their support to Mao and his party.

In recent years the west has had to contend with an even more complex shifting vision of Chinese reality. From 1949 to 1976, China conducted its daily life behind closed doors. The glimpses given to outsiders were too fleeting to allow a fair analysis of the realities of the communist regime in the People's Republic of China. The Cultural Revolution from 1966 to 1976 stunned western observers who were either horrified by the sight of millions of identically clad people mindlessly chanting slogans, or entranced at the thought of a great experiment in social engineering.

Only now since the fall of the 'Gang of Four' are western observers beginning to obtain additional pieces of the jigsaw puzzle with which to put together a picture of China. China itself is once more slowly and painfully opening its doors to the influence, beneficial or otherwise, of western culture and values.

The kaleidoscope of images that China has presented to the west has largely been the result of economic imbalances between China and the western world. Imagination has all too frequently made up for lack of information. Within a century the image of China has gone from one extreme to another. China, as well, has had violently contradictory perceptions of the west.

Is it possible that the 20th-century revolution in communications, bringing the most diverse and often antagonistic cultures closer together, will bring a greater understanding of the Chinese reality?

List of Chinese Dynasties

Palaeolithic	c.600,000—7000 BC
Neolithic	c.7000—1600 BC
Shang	c.1600—1027 BC
Western Zhou	1027—771 BC
Eastern Zhou	770—256 BC
Spring and Autumn Annals	722—481 BC
Warring States	480—221 BC
QIN	221—206 BC
FORMER (EASTERN) HAN	206 BC—25 AD
LATER (WESTERN) HAN	25—220
Three Kingdoms	220—265
Western Jin	265—316
Northern and Southern Dynasties	317—589
Northern Wei (Toba)	386—535
SUI	589—618
TANG	618—907
Five Dynasties and Ten Kingdoms	907—960
NORTHERN SONG	960—1127
Liao (Khitan)	907—1125
SOUTHERN SONG	1127—1279
Jin (Jurchen)	1115—1234
YUAN (MONGOL)	1279—1368
MING	1368—1644
QING (MANCHU)	1644—1911
Republic	1911—1949
PEOPLE'S REPUBLIC	1949—

The Great Wall at Badaling

VISITING CHINA

In the past eight years, China has experienced nothing short of a tourist tidal wave. Until the policy reversals following the arrest of the so-called Gang of Four in 1976, there was no tourist industry in China. Visiting foreign groups were restricted to a handful of carefully-screened, special interest parties and the ordinary traveller stood no chance of obtaining a visa.

However, within a remarkably short period of time, China's tourist industry has developed dramatically. A conference on tourism was held in early 1978 and an ambitious blueprint was produced. The *People's Daily* newspaper editorialized that the growth of China's tourist industry would promote better international understanding and help accumulate the much-needed foreign currency for economic expansion. In 1977, foreign tourists were limited to only a small number of 'open' cities, but now over 240 different areas have been opened to tourists — as far apart as Xinjiang in the northwest and Hainan Island off the southern coast of China. There has also been a trend to open more archaeological excavations and restore temples to encourage tourism. Last year China handled 17.8 million arrivals, most of them Overseas Chinese and visitors from Hong Kong. 1.37 million were foreign tourists.

The Chinese would be the first to admit to growing pains in their fast developing new industry. Nonetheless, what China offers today's tourist is a travel experience unlike any other. As in the days of Marco Polo, a traveller is regarded as an honoured guest, who must be given a full, if favourable, picture of the society he is visiting. Of course the Chinese are happy to show off their magnificent scenery and historical sights, but they also want to convey something of the way their society works, and of their economic and cultural progress. Itineraries are far less serious than a few years back — tours are not all factories and briefing sessions — but the Chinese still hope their foreign guests will not only sample the best of their food and entertainment, but also see their children being educated, watch their factories at work, and visit their communes.

When to Go

Within the almost four million square miles of China's vast territory it is hardly surprising to find immense variations in climate. Even generalizations about relatively small areas are difficult because of the effects of altitude and other local conditions. Before deciding on the best season to take a tour, it is worth checking carefully on the weather of each city on the itinerary. Of course, if you choose the most attractive season to visit a city, you also choose the time when tourist spots and hotels are most crowded.

As a basic guide, winters in the north are harsh: Beijing's average minimum temperature between December and March is only 23°F

(−5°C), and its maximum is around 32°F (0°C). If you go further north towards Harbin, or west into Inner Mongolia, it is much colder. By contrast, summer in the north can be uncomfortably hot and sticky. Temperatures in Beijing may soar over 100°F (38°C), while the average minimum between June and September is 75°F (25°C). The city has a rainy season in July and August. Spring and autumn are undoubtedly the best times for touring in the north, when you can expect less rain, clear skies and comfortable temperatures — the average maximum spring and autumn temperature in Beijing is 70°F (21°C).

Moving south, the Yangzi Valley area (which includes Shanghai) has semitropical conditions. Summers are long, hot and sticky with notoriously unpleasant conditions at Wuhan, Chongqing and Nanjing — cities which the Chinese have, with good reason, called the three furnaces. Winters are short and cold, with temperatures dipping below freezing, while spring and autumn are the most attractive seasons with cool nights and daytime highs in the mid 70s (around 24°C). Humidity remains high throughout the year — the average rainfall in Shanghai is 45 inches.

The subtropical south (Guangzhou is on the Tropic of Cancer) has a hot and humid six month period from April to September, with days of heavy rain (Guangzhou's average rainfall is 65 inches), but has a very pleasant dry, sunny autumn, with daytime temperatures in the 70s (around 24°C). Spring can be cloudy and wet, while the short winter from January to March produces some surprisingly chilly days.

What to Pack

Clothes Apart from mid-summer, when virtually everywhere open to foreign tourists is hot, most tour itineraries lead the tourist through several different weather zones. But people who decide to travel with several complete changes of wardrobe may find themselves with crippling excess baggage charges — the Chinese tend to be strict about their 20 kilo (44 lbs) baggage allowance. A more practical policy would be to plan on wearing layers that can be discarded or added to as the weather dictates.

The Chinese themselves are informal about dress, and will not expect tourists to dress formally for any occasion — even a banquet. So take casual, practical clothes, and strong, comfortable shoes — you are bound to be doing a lot of walking. Men need nothing smarter than a sports jacket and women can feel properly dressed wearing slacks on any occasion. Although the Chinese are becoming a little more adventurous with their own clothes, they are still offended by anything too flamboyant, and particularly by exposure of too much flesh. But in rapidly changing China even attitudes towards dress are relaxing. Nevertheless, women should leave their scanty clothes at home.

Winter in the north demands very heavy clothing — thick coats, sweaters, lined boots, gloves, and some form of headgear as protection against the biting wind. Hotels and tour buses are usually well heated, while museums, communes, and even some theatres and restaurants are not.

For summer anywhere in China keep clothes as light as possible — many of the places you visit will not be airconditioned. You may be sightseeing during the heat of the day, so take plenty of protection against the sun. A light raincoat is a wise addition to your luggage at any time.

You need bring only a few changes of clothing since hotel laundry everywhere is fast, cheap and efficient. Dry cleaning is possible, although it may be wiser to wait until you are home to get your most treasured clothes cleaned.

Food, Drink and Tobacco The days when tourists who wanted western liquor had to bring it with them are happily over. An ever increasing number of shops and Friendship Stores sell imported wines and spirits at prices which compare favourably with those in the west. Imported cigarettes are also sold, again at very reasonable prices. But if you want to play safe and bring along your own brands, a loosely enforced customs regulation allows you to import duty free 400 cigarettes and 2 bottles of liquor.

Coffee too is much more easily available now than it was when China first opened its doors to tourists — breakfast coffee in many hotels has become quite drinkable. But if you like it at all times of the day, bring some instant coffee (and powdered milk and sugar) and take advantage of the thermoses of hot water in your room and on the trains. Tea drinkers who prefer Indian rather than Chinese tea should also bring along their own.

There is no real need to bring your between-meal snacks with you. Many hotel shops sell Chinese peanuts, biscuits, chocolates, and sweets.

Film Many tourists bitterly regret not bringing more film with them. Film is available in China — Kodak claims over a hundred outlets — but the right type is not always available at the right time. You are, in fact, allowed to import up to six dozen rolls and 3000 feet of movie film, so why not bring enough to make sure you do not run out half way through China.

Medicine and Toiletries Bring any prescription medicines you know you will need, and a supply of medicines for your general health. Some of these drugs are available in China, but it is safer (and you will avoid loosing time shopping around) if you plan to be self-sufficient.

Apart from some imported cosmetics, most western produced toothpaste, shampoo, shaving cream and so on are not available, although there are of course Chinese brands of these items.

Electric Appliances Voltage may vary from region to region, but is mostly 220-240V. There is no consistency in the size or shape of plugs, so men would do better to bring normal razors and blades with them. Hotels and Friendship Stores sometimes have adapters, but if you really cannot live without a particular electric appliance, it would be best to bring a selection of adapters with you.

Reading Material Until the end of the seventies, almost the only reading material available to a tourist comprised copies of *China Reconstructs*, a magazine in a great many languages which puts China's positive socialist face forward and the press releases of the New China News Agency. Today, visitors to China can purchase copies of international magazines in the larger hotels as well as find some of the regional and international newspapers brought in from Hong Kong. Foreign books are also displayed for sale in hotel lobbies but look out for China's own English language daily newspaper, *China Daily*, and the many new English language paperbacks published in China.

Visas

Tourists travelling as part of a tour group enter China on a group visa — a single document listing all the members of the group. This visa is obtained by the tour operator on behalf of his clients. Individual visas can be obtained from Hong Kong travel agents or the Visa Office of the Ministry of Foreign Affairs of the PRC in Hong Kong or at Chinese Embassies in their respective foreign countries. These visas give access to 244 cities without further documentation. The fee for individual visas varies greatly from the different sources.

Health

CITS asks those who are unfit because of 'mental illness, contagious or serious chronic disease, disability, pregnancy, senility or physical handicap' not to take a China tour. Experience has shown this to be sound advice. A tour which is exhausting but stimulating for the fit becomes a gruelling experience for those who are not.

If you do become ill in China you are taken to the local hospital and given the best treatment available (not always of a standard that westerners are used to) and you will be put in a private room if possible. Costs — particularly of medicines — are high, so it is worth considering some form of health insurance.

There are no mandatory vaccination requirements, but gammaglobulin, up-to-date polio and tetanus shots, and B-encephalitis for those travelling between April and October are recommended. Anti-malaria precaution is useful for all areas south of Xi'an excluding Tibet. Anyone coming from a cholera-infected area should have an inoculation.

Customs

Customs officials treat tour groups gently and you need not expect long holdups in the customs hall. On entering China you fill out a customs declaration form, a duplicate of which must be kept and produced again when you leave. You are asked to list items such as cameras, watches,

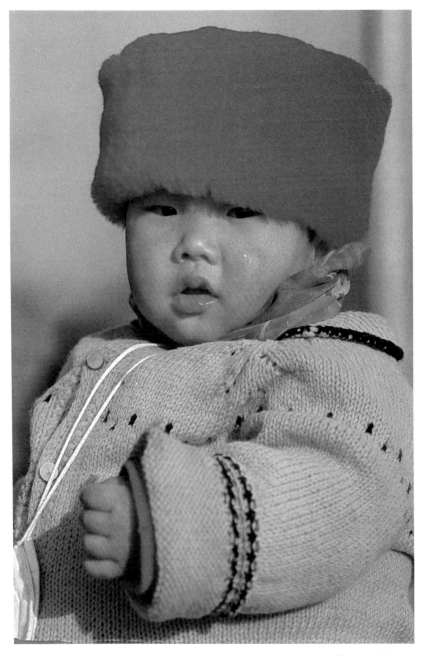

Winter in Beijing.

jewellery, radios and recorders that you are bringing into China. These listed items are not to be sold or given away while you are in China, and the customs officer may ask to see them when you leave.

Antiques up to the value of RMB 10,000 may be exported as long as they have a red wax seal on them indicating that the authorities approve of the exportation. Customs may ask to see the special receipt you are given when buying an antique.

China International Travel Service

Although an ever increasing number of foreigners in China are coming independently or use the services of other agencies, many still come to China with the help of these especially attentive hosts — the staff of the ubiquitous CITS (China International Travel Service), also known as Lüxingshe — who look after every aspect of the tour. They plan the itinerary, allocate hotels, make travel arrangements, devise daily sightseeing programmes, arrange meals, provide guide-interpreters and much more besides.

Even though CITS is now in a position to offer the foreign tourist a wider

Huating Temple, Western Hills Park, Kunming

choice in matters of hotel accommodation, transport and overall tour itineraries, the mind still reels at the unenviable task which faces CITS whose job it is to manipulate China's limited hotel and transport facilities to accommodate all their foreign visitors. Understandably, once CITS personnel have laid their plans they are unlikely to want to alter them at the request of the tourists, or even tour operators. China's tourist facilities simply cannot cope with a greater degree of flexibility for the moment.

CITS doubtlessly determines in advance the shape of a tour (the order that places will be visited and number of days spent in each) but these details are usually not confirmed to the foreign visitors until they arrive in China. Tourists and tour operators are also kept in the dark on other aspects of their tour — until arriving in a city no-one knows for sure where their group will stay or what they will be doing. Perhaps this way of going about things is entirely alien to the experienced western traveller, but it is one which at present has to be readily accepted in China.

Guides

CITS is generous with its guiding services. From the moment a group steps into China, a CITS guide-interpreter will usually meet them and stick by their side through to the final departure lounge. This national guide is joined by at least one local guide at each city the group visits. Standards of guiding vary considerably. Your guides may be knowledgeable and fluent in English. They may, on the other hand, have done little travelling within China, have scant knowledge of the area where they are guiding, and have had little chance to practise their English. But more important, they are almost universally helpful, tireless in their attempts to answer questions, and make good travelling companions.

Daily Programmes

Like all enthusiastic hosts, CITS expects its guests to keep up a cracking pace. A day which may start at dawn with a visit to a market could lead on to a morning's sightseeing, an afternoon visit to a school, a shopping session, and not wind up till ten in the evening after a visit to a local opera. Much is expected of the foreign guests' stamina. You may find yourself climbing the 392 steps of Dr Sun Yat-sen's Mausoleum in Nanjing in mid summer temperatures, travelling in an unheated jeep along a frozen riverbed in the depths of the Mongolian winter, or sitting on hard benches in an airless stadium watching a four-hour acrobatic show.

To get the most out of your China programme you must be prepared to sometimes forego a lengthy break for a shower or a pre-dinner martini. But CITS guides are far from being severe taskmasters. If it all gets too much, they are quite willing to let you rest all day in your hotel, or skip an expedition to wander off on your own.

Travelling inside China

The CITS hosts look after all travel arrangements for their foreign guests. They select the date, time and type of transport, make reservations, see to necessary security clearances, and ensure that luggage gets from the hotel onto the appropriate train or plane. It is only left for the tourists to pay their own excess baggage charges.

Most foreign tourists travel the long distances between China's major cities by air, and the shorter intercity distances on the train.

18th-century mosque, Turpan

Air Travel CAAC (Civil Aviation Authority of China), which once had the monopoly on domestic flights (now a number of independent domestic airlines are appearing) has greatly expanded its services recently. But there is still an element of adventure in flying within China. Flights may be cancelled if bad weather is forecast, reserved seats may mysteriously be filled by others, and sometimes aircraft simply do not turn up. CAAC fly an interesting array of aircraft on internal flights, ranging from Russian Ilyushins and Antonov turboprops to British Trident jets and newly acquired Boeing 767s.

You will experience few of the frills associated with commercial airlines in the west. Inflight service has a distinctive CAAC quality to it. Demurely dressed airhostesses serve light refreshments together with gifts of keyrings, fans, vases, or perhaps a butterfly papercut. During longer flights planes may make a special stopover for crew and passengers to have a more substantial meal at an airport restaurant. Airports, apart from the new international-style one at Beijing which opened in January 1980, tend to be spartan places with a minimum of services.

There are plans afoot to bring CAAC more in line with other airlines — some personnel are being trained in Japan, for example — and booking systems are to be streamlined and computerized. But however welcome increased efficiency will be, there are bound to be China travellers who will regret the passing of days when shy airhostesses carried large kettles of water up the aisles to refill passenger tea cups.

Trains Most foreign tourists enjoy the long distance train trips, however reluctant they may be at first to embark on such a journey. 'Soft class' — the class reserved for foreigners and high ranking officials (although other classes are available too) — combines old world charm with comfort and efficiency. Clean white embroidered seat covers, an endless supply of hot water and green tea, regular mopping of the floors, effective heating in winter, and dining cars which can produce adequate Chinese meals (beer, and sometimes Chinese wine, are available) — all add up to ideal conditions for sitting back and watching China's diverse countryside speed by. Overnight passengers are comfortably housed in velvet curtained four-bunked compartments, with a potted plant in each. Each car has washing and toilet facilities that are an improvement on many of their western counterparts. Another plus for Chinese trains, not always mirrored in the west, is their punctuality — to be on time in China it is still safest to travel by train.

Tour Buses For sightseeing CITS has a range of tour buses. Foreign groups are usually put in luxury 40-seater Hino buses imported from Japan, equipped with airconditioning, heating that works, and an effective public address system. Smaller groups may be allocated 16-seater Toyota buses — very adequate although designed for Japanese-sized passengers. Occasionally, tourists may find themselves touring in older, unsprung Chinese-made buses.

Taxis For moving around town on your own, taxis provide an easy answer. They are cheap by international standards, and drivers are usually happy to wait while you shop, sightsee or have a meal in a local restaurant. Fares are worked out on a time and distance formula, and in some cities meters are becoming the norm.

Taxis generally do not cruise the streets looking for fares, Fleets of taxis — either imported Toyotas or more characterful, if old-fashioned, Shanghai-branded and produced vehicles — serve the major hotels in all the most frequented open cities. In these cities there will probably be a special desk in your hotel lobby which arranges taxis. Restaurants, clubs and tourist stores should also call one for you. Whichever city you are in, your CITS escort should be able to arrange a hired car and driver if you want to make a special excursion.

Public Transport Only the most enterprising short-stay visitors would set out to find their way round on public transport. No doubt there are many efficient bus and trolleybus services in China's cities, but it is difficult to come to grips with the systems at once, especially if you do not speak Chinese. Route maps are in Chinese and, since the fare is based on distance travelled, you should be able to say in Chinese where you are going. You may also have to muster considerable strength to push yourself both on and off the bus.

Hotels

Foreign travellers come to China for its magnificent scenery, rich cultural traditions or ambitious modern social experiments, but generally not for its hotels. This is slowly changing as a new generation of international-class hotels goes up in the larger cities. Still, any visitor is likely to have varied experiences of accommodation, and nobody is immune from the possibility of a classic Chinese hotel horror story.

But looked at from another perspective, it is no wonder that China has only just recently built up a small network of international-standard hotels — their tourist industry is, after all, only eight years old. Those involved in the fledgling industry are only too aware that improvements are needed. As the Director of CITS put it a few years ago, 'there are too few hotels, a shortage of modern equipment, and hotel management is not up to standard.'

The Chinese have already shown every sign of learning fast about the essential needs of their foreign guests. There are already more airconditioners and icemakers, more hotel coffee bars where guests can get a drink or snack after the hotel kitchens have closed down (which they usually do around 8pm), more English-speaking staff, more souvenir shops.

But at this stage it is unreasonable to expect China to match the standards of the best international chains. Why not rather set out to enjoy the individual charm of the hotels as they are now? For example there are the grand old hotels of Shanghai, built during the twenties and thirties, when the city was the 'Paris of the East'. Although many have been thoroughly refurbished inside, while keeping their architectural exterior intact, the art-déco mood of the Peace Hotel (once the famous Cathay Hotel, an essential part of any Far East traveller's itinerary) still retains much of its former opulence and charm. Then there is the quiet old-fashioned comfort of the state guesthouses, until recently reserved for high ranking Chinese officials and guests of state, but now opened to tourists. Or there are the Russian-built hotels of the fifties, with their vast suites, high ceilings, marble halls and bulbous furniture, and the later high-rise hotels the Chinese built themselves — strictly utilitarian, often shoddily finished, but sometimes superbly positioned.

International-style hotels have come to China, and their advent means travel in China has lost a small part of its charm and individuality.

Hotel Facilities A typical standard room has twin beds, a cupboard, desk, chair and bathroom ensuite. You will find a few trimmings —

Kazak yurt, near Ürümqi

notepaper, mugs, an inkwell, a comb, a desk calendar — and now radios, televisions, and refrigerators are increasingly common. Thermos flasks of pre-boiled water are invariably provided and can be used to make tea (green tea is usually offered) or coffee (you should bring your own). You should not drink tap water anywhere in China.

Room service is usually run from a service desk on each floor of the hotel. The staff at these counters try hard to be accommodating — they collect and deliver laundry, keep the thermoses filled, put through long distance calls, and may even do minor tailoring repairs, polish shoes, deliver ice, and babysit.

The days when foreigners could safely leave their rooms unlocked are unfortunately over so it is wise to ask at the service counter for your room key.

Most large hotels have banking, postage and cable facilities on the spot. Many have coffee shops and bars that stay open until reasonably late hours, souvenir shops, and hairdressers which may offer the irresistable opportunity of a head massage.

Money

Renminbi and Currency Certificates Chinese currency is called *renminbi* (meaning people's currency) and is abbreviated to RMB. The standard unit is *yuan* (referred to as *kuai* in everyday speech). The yuan or kuai is divided into 10 *jiao* (referred to as *mao*) and 100 *fen*. 10 fen make one mao and 10 mao make one kuai. Yuan (kuai) and jiao (mao) are available in note forms and fen as small nickel coins. With the introduction of foreign exchange certificates in May 1980, tourists have not been given RMB by banks handling exchange transactions. Currency certificates can be used anywhere although their official use is for payment in hotels, Friendship Stores and official receipts. This led to a large black market exchange between RMB and FEC. In September 1986 it was officially announced that FECs were to be phased out in the near future. Shortly thereafter a postponement was announced, so the RMB-FEC question is still open.

Foreign Currency There is no limit to the amount of foreign currency you can bring into China. You should keep all your exchange memos — the bank may demand to see these when you come to reconvert your currency certificates on leaving China.

All major freely negotiable currencies can be exchanged for currency certificates at branches of the Bank of China in hotels and stores. The rates of exchange fluctuate with the international money market.

Cheques and Credit Cards All the major European, American and Japanese travellers cheques are accepted. Major international credit cards are now also quite freely accepted in shops and hotels of major cities. It is possible to cash American Express Travellers Cheques in 52 cities.

Tipping is never required, although it is beginning to be expected in major cities.

Shopping

Some foreigners come to China believing that it will prove a shopper's paradise, while others have been told there is nothing worth buying. A truer picture probably lies half-way between these extremes. Unless you live in Hong Kong where there is a wide range of China-produced goods at highly competitive prices, you are bound to come across some things during your China tour which seem ludicrously inexpensive. At the same time, the Chinese have grown very aware of their spend-happy tourist market and you should not expect a bargain at every turn.

Sword Peak Pond, Stone Forest, Yunnan

There is never a problem finding shopping opportunities during a China tour — CITS is highly accommodating to foreign visitors anxious to rid themselves of their sought-after foreign currency, and will lead you to tempting stores of different kinds.

Friendship Stores No China tour would be complete without a visit to a Friendship Store. These shops were originally established specifically to sell export goods to foreign visitors. The biggest is in Beijing (catering to the capital's growing foreign community as well as to tourists) and you will find scaled-down versions in most cities open to foreigners. Friendship Stores still offer many products that do not circulate in the local economy — better quality silks, crafts, jewellery and so on — but they also now stock goods found in local stores.

There are advantages to Friendship Store shopping — the counters are uncrowded, the sales staff understand a little English, and the merchandise is likely to be the best quality available. But there are drawbacks too — prices may be heavily marked up (sometimes an identical article can be bought for half the price in a local store), there are not many everyday items for sale, and constant shopping in a rarified Friendship Store atmosphere deprives you of the more exciting experience of shopping with the bustle of Chinese shoppers around you.

Local Department Stores China's new consumer-oriented mood is conspicuously evident in all city department stores, nowadays filled with so much more than the bare essentials displayed a few years ago.

A visit to a major city department store is a must, not simply to compare prices with those in Friendship Stores, but to get a feel of everyday Chinese life. The biggest department stores are in Shanghai, the city with more than 24,000 shops and a justified reputation as China's best shopping centre. The vast Number One Department Store on Nanjing Road, constantly packed with enthusiastic shoppers casting a discerning eye over new stock, claims to offer over 36,000 different commodities, serving 100,000 customers a day.

But whichever city you are in, you will find expeditions to the local shops far less complicated than you might imagine. There is, after all, no bargaining to be done, and prices are usually marked in Arabic numerals. In any case, Chinese shopkeepers are generally honest, so that you need never feel you are being cheated. You may find you attract a crowd — particularly in less visited spots — but there is certainly no hostility, just straightforward curiosity.

In some parts of China certain items are still rationed — silks, cottons, or tobacco for example — and you need ration coupons to buy them in the local stores. Your CITS guide may, with difficulty, be able to get hold of coupons for you, but it is probably easier to abandon the purchase and try the Friendship Store.

Tourist Shops Tours of handicraft factories invariably end up at a small shop selling samples of the articles produced there. You may stumble on some unusual pieces here, but be conscious that you are considered a captive market and that prices may be inflated.

Small souvenir shops have sprung up at all the main tourist tramping grounds — in hotel lobbies, cunningly secreted in temples and garden pavilions, beneath the Great Wall, and even in the depths of the Ming Tombs. There are generalizations to be made on the quality of goods sold,

Exhibition Centre, Chengdu

which range from the shoddy and overpriced to some attractive and unique souvenirs.

With the return of private enterprise to China, you may find hawkers at popular tourist spots selling paintings, maps, and an enterprising assortment of souvenirs. Here, well away from the realms of fixed prices, you may be able to strike a good bargain.

Some Shopping Suggestions

Arts and Crafts No traveller could fail to note China's efforts to modernize and promote her traditional craft industries. Visits to arts and crafts 'factories' and 'research institutes' figure large on any itinerary, and there can be few tourists able to resist the array of handicrafts enticingly displayed in hotel lobby shops and Friendship Stores. There is jewellery incorporating precious and semi-precious stones — jade, rose quartz, lapis lazuli, diamonds — and carved ivory, cloisonné, lacquerwork, papercuts, Chinese lanterns, miniature cork carvings, scroll paintings, clay figurines, sandalwood fans, two-sided silk embroidery, exquisitely hand-embroidered linen, rugs — the list is almost endless.

Some handicrafts are regionally produced and best bought in that particular area — silk in Suzhou or Wuxi for example, or basketware in

Chengdu — so find out from your guide the speciality of the area, and snap up anything you like at once — the same items may not crop up again in arts and crafts stores in other cities.

Antiques If you come to China expecting a startling array of antique shops to rummage through, you will be disappointed. The government keeps a tight control over the marketing of antiques, and only licensed shops in a few cities are allowed to sell to foreign tourists. Beijing and Shanghai are the biggest outlets, with smaller shops in cities such as

Gate-tower,
Great Wall, Jiayuguan

Nanjing, Wuxi and Guangzhou. Only 'antiques' which are *less* than 120 years old appear on the shelves of these shops, and some of the best buys have already been snapped up by earlier discerning foreign visitors.

Do not expect any exceptional bargains — the Chinese are very aware of what they are selling. Prices on Liulichang, Beijing's old and famous antiques street, would match up to those anywhere in the world, and sceptics point out that now that the street's facelift has been completed prices have crept even higher.

Although you are unlikely to stumble over any rarities, China's antique stores still make delightful browsing for the layman, particularly if you are lucky enough to encounter one of the older members of staff with a deep knowledge of his merchandise.

Furs, Silk and Cashmere Furs and suedes can be excellent value, particularly mink, leopardskin, astrakhan, rabbit and sheepskin. The widest range can be found in Shanghai and Beijing, where you may also have coats and jackets tailor-made.

Cashmere prices seem ludicrously low to westerners, and nowadays the design and colour of sweaters, gloves and scarves are more acceptable to the western eye.

China's famous silks can be bought by the yard as well as already made up into blouses, often highly embroidered, luxurious nightwear, jackets and scarves. The range of colours and the design of printed silks have improved enormously, while prices remain half those you would expect to pay in the west.

Some More Bargains Part of the enjoyment of shopping in China is in seeking out your own particular bargains. So numerous are they that only time limits the scope for an enthusiastic bargain hunter. Among the discoveries that other visitors have already made are: tea, Chinese caviar, saffron, children's clothes, toys, stationery, art supplies (especially brushes), 'kung fu' shoes, 'Mao' hats, waxed paper umbrellas, luggage, books, scissors and Chinese musical instruments.

Communications

China has efficient international communications systems so it is a relatively simple and speedy business to make long-distance telephone calls or send cables. Most major hotels also have access to telex facilities. Airmail letter and cards *do* reach their destination, although they may take some time to do so. If you are thinking about sending any large purchases home, bear in mind that while shipping costs are average, crating charges are high, and the crate may not arrive for many months.

Points of Entry

In 1985 China's points of entry for tourists greatly increased. For the adventurous, the Karakorum Highway — linking Pakistan and Xinjiang in northwestern China — and the Kathmandu-Lhasa Highway — linking Nepal and Tibet are now travelled by the patient and hardy. Once weekly regular flights come into Kunming from Rangoon, Burma (CAAC) and Bangkok, Thailand (CAAC). Boats can be taken from Japan and Hong Kong. International flights arrive daily from numerous starting points into Beijing and Shanghai. The newly established Hong Kong based airline, Dragon Air, is now flying regular flights on Boeing 737-200s into Guangzhou (Canton), Xiamen, Guilin and Hangzhou and by February 1987 will have flights to Nanjing, Tianjin, Kunming, Dalian, Fuzhou, Xi'an, Chengdu, Haikou and Shantou. And of course for the inveterate train lover there is still the Trans-Siberian Railway leaving twice weekly from Moscow.

Picking tea, Hangzhou

FOOD IN CHINA

A millenium-old Chinese legend has it that a virtuous citizen of Hangzhou went to heaven, where he was greeted by the Judge of Rewards.

'You are a good man,' said the Judge, 'so I shall return you to earth rich and powerful.'

'But I *don't* want to be a rich man or powerful,' said the citizen. 'All I want is a regular supply of West Lake fish and bamboo shoots, some Dragon Well tea, and to pass through life without worries.'

The Judge replied, 'I'm sorry. I can give you all the money and the power that you want. But this peaceful, happy, simple life.....well, that's more than *any* god can provide.'

The simple life of great cuisine..... Most foreigners making their first trip to China expect either a) that Chinese dine on great 18-course banquets every night; or b) that they live a frugal life of rice — plain rice.

The truth is somewhere in between. Banquets are certainly not unknown, especially for official dignitaries, or bureaucrats entertaining their important guests from abroad. But most people in China eat either rice or noodles (the former for the south and central parts of China, the latter for the north), vegetables, offal, sometimes fowl or pork, less frequently beef, and if in the right area, fish. Diets are fairly nutritious, especially in the tropical and subtropical south. But, unless presented with the most exceptional dignitaries or on special occasions, hardly sumptuous.

With tourists, though, the People's Republic of China has gradually — if sometimes reluctantly — come to see that a true curiosity about Chinese food and a sense of adventure generally, mean that they must provide the finest. Or at least the finest which they *believe* that foreign guests would enjoy. No tour group in Guangdong, for example, would be treated to dog or snakemeat, which are considered delicacies in the region. But recently no tourist who has requested to eat in one of the two 'wild animal' restaurants has been denied a meal. No guide of China International Travel Service would deign to seat his Beijing tourists in the loud, hilarious, rambunctious *downstairs* section of the Yunnanese restaurant Kangle; he will instead try to take them to the more sedate upstairs private rooms. With enough effort and persistence, though, the ordinary tourist can sit downstairs and enjoy the frivolity, pointing to the dishes he may like to try.

Unfortunately, as the PRC has come to realize that foreigners wish exciting imaginative dishes, they have begun to eschew the usual fresh good fare of the regions, and have brought out instead set 'banquets' which are as expensive (and not half as good) as in the Chinese restaurants of Hong Kong.

Obviously, those who love their Chinese food have to fight against the banquet syndrome, which has recently become almost a disease among

Chinese restauranteurs. Overcharging per se is never done, but inflated prices for mediocre fare in isolated dining rooms doesn't give any visitor a good appetite.

Fortunately, China International Travel Service guides are so brilliantly well-schooled as translators that the persistent — nay, resolute and indefatigable — tourist who loves his fine food may just be able to arrange to have some extraordinary meals obtainable nowhere else in the world.

There is a reason why China is so hesitant about bringing out its great dishes. During the Cultural Revolution, chefs were no less immune than bureaucrats from the political radicalism of the times. In 1979, when this writer was in China for the first time, the reinstatement of professional chefs and cooks was taking place, and the stories of how they had been demoted to dishwashers, while the cadres took over the *wok* and stove, were pretty horrifying. Especially to a people for whom food, as Confucius said, 'is the first happiness.'

In 1966, the food of China began to slide into a nadir from which it has just recovered. *The Masses Cookbook,* published in that year, introduced a 'new cuisine' with special emphasis on economy and ease of preparation. The simplest methods (i.e. stir-frying) and the simplest ingredients (i.e. vegetables) were the answer for the masses. And only recently has it come out that the 'Gang of Four' and their clique had closed down Beijing's most impressive restaurant, Fangshan, to the masses, so they could instead enjoy their own frolics in the great surrounding park. (The restaurant and park were reopened in 1979, one is happy to report.)

What saved Chinese cuisine in the long run was not only the love and great tradition of fine cooking; but — as our honourable citizen of the legend above knew — great cooking means basically *simple* cooking. But not as self-consciously simple as *The Masses Cookbook* would have them believe. More as the 18th-century gourmet-poet Yuan Mei pointed out when he hired a cook. 'I once said to the cook,' wrote Yuan, "I can understand your producing great results with rare materials. What astonishes me is that, out of a couple of eggs you have made a dish that nobody else can make." He replied to me, "The cook who works on only a small scale lacks grace. Good cooking doesn't depend on the size of the dish or the cost of the ingredient. If one has the art, then a piece of celery or salted cabbage can be made into a delicacy. If one has not the art, then all the delicacies and rarities of land, sea or sky are to no avail." '

The Chinese had — and again have — the art.

Where to find this art today? The best food, the ultimate *haute cuisine* of the Chinese' has always been in Guangdong, the province of the Cantonese. Gourmets pinpoint various villages from which the art supposedly had its roots; but these legends are apocryphal. More important is the *natural* element. Guangdong is tropical *and* subtropical. With a coastline 1000 miles long, with fruits, teas, birds, beef and seafood commonplace, with a multitude of mushrooms and with a traditional reverence for freshness, Guangdong has a greater variety of recipes than any other single province in China.

Freshness is everything to the Cantonese. So is quick cooking; not much long broiling, or barbecueing as in the north. And no simmering for hours with spices and herbs as in the west. The Cantonese steam fish (no frying oils here); they stir-fry or quick-fry their vegetables. And as for meats, they roast them. One of their rare barbecued dishes, the pork, is beautifully reddish on the outside, while white and juicy inside.

The Cantonese never ever use an excess of ingredients or sauces (though the side-dish sauces are plentiful enough: black bean sauce, garlic, ginger, rich smooth oyster sauce, lobster sauce, lemon sauce). They use the most concentrated chicken *bouillon* as the basis of soups. Most of all, they preserve that special elegance, whether it be in the incomparable early morning *dim sum* (hors d'oeuvres), roast duck, or even in all-vegetable dishes, with their mushrooms, fungus, gingko nuts and beansprouts.

There probably isn't a major city in China without one Cantonese-style restaurant. But during the winter Guangzhou City stands in a class by itself. As mentioned above, the city has two 'wild animal' restaurants, which serve an intriguing selection of dog, cat, snake, guinea pig and wildcat. Not to everybody's taste, of course. But to the Cantonese, these foods make a winter of dish content.

Yet Cantonese is but one of a large number of schools of Chinese cooking. To the pre-Revolution Chinese, every province, every district, and sometimes every town, had its specialities. So vast is the country that no one school of cooking could be claimed to be quintessentially Chinese. After the revolution, each of the *major* schools were allowed to function.

How many schools of cooking are there? Classically, there are only five definable schools .

Besides Cantonese cooking, there is also the Fujianese school, the Henan school (in north central China), the Shandong school (which is far better known as the Beijing school) and the Sichuan school. To this can be added the Jiangsu and Yangzhou cooking, in Shanghai.

None of them has the universality of appeal of Cantonese cooking....but all have unusual, often brilliant tastes.

One must start in Beijing, for a number of reasons. First, because Beijing has at least one restaurant devoted to each school of Chinese cooking. Second, because, as the imperial capital for over 700 years, Beijing created special recipes to please the imperial tastes, despite the virtual aridity of the region.

If truth be known, the northern region of China has never been known for its important food products. In the great steppe area, sheep is the main livestock; and rice is unknown, with wheat noodles and dumplings the staple. Yet on the coastline, the province of Shandong has its long history of great sailors and fine seafood. High up on the cliffs, swallows' nest is harvested for bird's nest soup. And the chefs of Shandong were so well-trained that the Manchus, who took over the capital in 1644, soon made use of their talents for the Imperial Palace.

The result has been a most fortunate one, as visitors to Beijing soon discover. At one end, the diner can go to Donglaishun Restaurant, in Dongfeng Market, sit downstairs, and enjoy a basically Mongolian meal with all the visiting Mongolians of the region. Most important is Mongolian hotpot , with at least 100 slices of millimetre-thin lamb, plates of celery, cabbage, spinach leaves, and a charcoal-burning pot in which one dips the ingredients, then coats them with a do-it-yourself sauce. You mix the sauce from palettes of vinegar, mustard paste, Sichuan hot pepper, bean paste, ginger, garlic, parsley, green onions and sesame oil. Or you could try the shashlick of lamb, or exotica like sheephead in casserole or camel hump. (For the latter, at least four days' notice must be given.)

At the other end of the Beijing-Shandong cuisine is the aforementioned Fangshan Restaurant, with its imperial dishes which are...well, rather heavy: fried chicken with water chestnuts, live steamed fish, and deep-fried laminated pork, coated with flour, egg, soy and ginger in a kind of fatback 'sandwich'.

But the most important classical dish, the apex of an emperor's meal, was the Beijing ('Peking') duck. And in Beijing, three or four restaurants serve not only the duck skin (the most important part of the fowl), but full all-duck dinners: tongue, feet, breast, liver (served nicely on dumplings made with duck skin outside, minced meat inside).

As in Cantonese cuisine, Beijing Shandong food has its fine winter specials: mutton and spring onions, great white cabbages, fine apples. And a special winter duck too. Winter duck is seen on all the street corners hanging in the windows, stretched out like lovely auburn tapestries with crispy skin and a delicate aroma. The reason they're stretched so thin is that traditionally the most salubrious breezes are considered to be those coming from the winter steppes. And the only method of absorbing these currents into the taste of the duck is to hang the flattened-out birds in the air for at least a month. One wonders whether, in honour of the occasion, Mongolian gourmets include wind-tasters who can tell from which latitude the duck was from!

But Beijing itself has more than Mongolian and imperial food. Tour guides may have to do some research, but they can easily dig up samples of the most interesting cuisines within the city: there are Hunan, Moslem, Shanghai, Shanxi, Sichuan and Yunnan restaurants, as well as pure Shandong food, with brilliant carp, crispy chicken steamed and then fried in oil, or braised fish.

One moves now to the great dishes of the Yangzi basin: the Jiangsu and Yangzhou schools, notably present in Hangzhou, Suzhou and Nanjing.

Shanghai, like New York, has no real cuisine of its own. But as the melting pot of China, as the most outward-looking and cosmopolitan town, it has taken some of the best dishes and made them into its own.

To some, the food of this region is a little oily, a little greasy at times. Shanghai people braise their food with a questionable triad of soy, wine and sugar which, if cooked exactly, turns into a delicious concentrated gravy. If not, they turn into a rather thick sauce as found in the Shanghai Old Town restaurants, where the 'purest' Shanghai foods are obtained.

For this writer, the food of Hangzhou is the nonpareil of food outside of Guangdong Province. It was the same for Marco Polo, who raved about 'the abundance of victuals, wild game, fowls, vegetables and huge pears, lake fish, plump and tasty, spiced rice wine.....' all of which are still available.

Hangzhou is the home of many wonderful dishes which should never be missed: 'beggar's' chicken covered with special clay and stuffed with lotus stuffing (this dish is at its best in late summer, when the West Lake lotuses are freshly picked). The shrimp and rice crust is fine, as is a stewed pork, named for the poet Su Dongpo (who hated pork, so braised and steamed it until it reached the consistency of beancurd), and the eels are marvellous. For breakfast, stay out of the hotels on the tourist side of the West Lake and go to Kuiyuan Restaurant which has the delicious Hangzhou 'cat's ear' noodles. And for tea — the famous fragrant Dragon Well tea which *smothers* the city in May — go to the West Lake teahouses.

But for the ultimate Hangzhou food, the finest classical dishes, one must inevitably go to Shanwaishan inside the Botanical Gardens. No English menu, but the specialities are easily translated. An egg and red bean dish called 'Lingering Snow on "Intersecting" Bridge', a seasonal soup with the water vegetable, *chuncai*, found only in Hangzhou and taken from the West Lake, fried eels and snow shrimps, and finally some soya beans fried in oil with a skin as thin, light and delicate as the best Viennese strudel. Hangzhou is one town where one should avoid the hotel restaurants at any cost.

Suzhou is nearby, but has totally different specialities. Here is 'squirrel' fish which literally chatters when a sauce is poured over the top of it. And here are the misnamed 'Shanghai crabs' which come crawling out in late autumn. But Suzhou is best known for its pastries, and these *must* be tried, in the early morning, at Huangtianyuan, whose history goes back 300 years. In the glass cases are 100 different sweets, made with red rice, egg yolk, cabbage juice, cocoa, red bean paste, walnuts, pinenuts, sugar and preserved fruits. Suzhou is also known for its splendid food-carving. And nowhere is it better than at Suzhou Hotel, for a costly but very stylish, delicious banquet.

Ironically, should one ask in either Shanghai or Beijing what their ultimate *best* restaurant might be, they will choose the restaurant featuring

Sichuan dishes. Both the Sichuan Restaurants in Beijing and Shanghai are praised for their sumptuous surroundings and good hot garlicky food. This writer prefers the more down-to-earth Emei Restaurant in Beijing (though Craig Claibourne of the *New York Times* felt that the Sichuan Restaurant there was one of the best in the world). At either place, as well as in Chengdu itself, Sichuan food is in a class by itself.....unless you don't like garlic and hot peppers, in which case 'tis better to leave the food alone. (To spare the tourist's feelings, both restaurants in Beijing and Shanghai will moderate the spices. It isn't worth the effort, as the food is blandly boring without them.) Sichuan Province is blessed with good rice, bamboo, wheat, corn, fruits of all sorts, and seafood from the great rivers of the valleys. They also believe in extremes: very sour, very hot, sweet or salty, with their own native salt, pepper, star anise, fennel seed and coriander. They don't like Cantonese stir-frying, but prefer steaming, simmering and smoking. And the smoked Sichuan duck (if *exactly* right, not too dry, not too moist) is as fine as Beijing duck.

Hunanese dishes, so popular in America right now, are something like Sichuanese. But the portions are larger, and more ginger than pepper is used. Few tourists get up to Changsha in Hunan. But a good idea of the food from Mao Zedong's own province can be had by visiting the joyous catacombs of Beijing's Xiangjiang Restaurant.

Henan food is rich, very tasty, and is little known to the west. Those fortunate enough to go to Zhengzhou, the capital, should insist on some of the specials here: kidney, which is fried in pieces the size of a walnut, and tastes tender and crisp at the same time, and the sweet-and-sour sauces for fish. And even more special is the 'Monkey Head' mushrooms. These can be had only in Henan Province, and they are as delicate as truffles when cooked with chicken or fish. (The Henan school is also the home of the famous bears' paws. But as the bears are a somewhat endangered species, one prefers not to recommend this.)

The last of the supposed *great* schools of cooking is Fujian. This writer knows few westerners (or Chinese) who really *like* Fujian food. The best restaurants are in Taiwan, near the Great Circle in the old section of Taibei. Here, one can feast on soups all day and all night, for the great Fujianese dishes are all in light clear soups, often made with pig offal or other questionable delicacies.

Far more to western tastes is Chaozhou food, from Shantou, to the south of Fujian. This is a gutsy hearty cuisine, with a penchant for the thickest sharks' fin soup (virtually a stew), superb goose doused in soy sauce, excellent seafood, dried blood (somewhat akin to Neapolitan blood pancakes) and a dozen varieties of sweet bird's nest.

From the extremes of China's borders come some of the most interesting dishes, though it's difficult to find them. At the newly opened tourist spots, the Chinese guides prefer to keep visitors inside the hotels. For example, none of the regular tours in Lhasa get to go to a Tibetan restaurant. Yet one should certainly try to eat the staple dish, *tsampa* — roasted barley mixed into yak-butter tea, rolled into balls and eaten with the fingers. Yak butter is rather bitter, incidentally, almost fermented, and the tea is not especially pleasant. However, it complements a meal of yak meat, fruit and yak cheese.

Uygur family, Turpan

Then there's Yunnan, recently opened and fascinating in terms of food. Visitors should ask for the mutton banquet; no fewer than 34 cold dishes are made from mutton. (The 35th dish is a hot soup.) Other specials (which are also available in Beijing at Kangle Restaurant) are much better than the little-known reputation of Yunnan would suggest: the most famous dish is the Yunnan ham, which should come frozen to the table. But piping hot are the 'crossing-over-bridge' noodles, a dish of previously uncooked noodles and condiments dumped into scalding water. They also have a chicken so soft that the bones can be eaten, and delicious egg soups, filled with shrimp, cucumber, pungent smoked fish...

Inhabitants of Inner Mongolia, in the far north, live mainly on mutton, and hotpot . With luck, one can have a meal inside a Mongolian yurt, with steaming plates of lamb and great bowls of fermented mare's milk. And in Ürümqi, in China's northwest province of Xinjiang, every street has different kinds of foods for the different minority groups which inhabit the region. Regular guides might not approve — the 'civilised' Chinese prefer their own simple restaurants, rather than eating ethnic — but you might be able to find the great dishes of the Hui (Chinese Moslems) here on your own: flat bread, mutton, and tea. Usually if you find a Hui restaurant, you can have a basic all-lamb meal which is a delight: typical might be hot lamb, egg with lamb, fish in red sauce, fried lamb with a bland sauce, fried duck liver and beancurd with egg.

Guangzhou.

Eating anywhere in China, then, can be such a zesty, tasty experience that words do no justice. Yet one must still persist in eating outside of the hotels. To the Chinese, foreign guests should be treated only to 'the best', and this best means unadventurous food in unadventurous surroundings. A few years ago, foreigners weren't even *allowed* in non-hotel restaurants. Today they are allowed. In time, the authorities might even encourage visitors to be adventurous. Today, adventure is a necessary adjunct to superb eating.

THE NORTHEAST

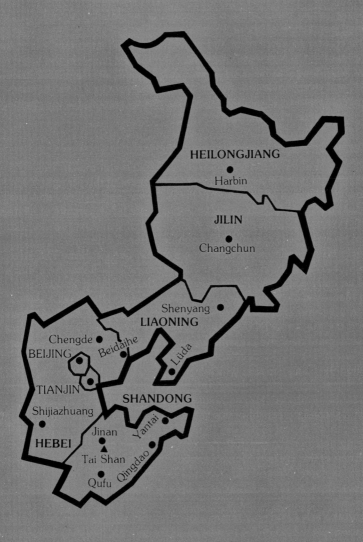

HEILONGJIANG

• Harbin

JILIN

• Changchun

Shenyang •

LIAONING

Chengde • Lüda

BEIJING • Beidaihe

TIANJIN

Shijiazhuang

SHANDONG

Jinan Yantai •

HEBEI

Tai Shan ▲ Qingdao •

Qufu

The Northeast

The northeast dominates the People's Republic of China both politically and economically. Over a quarter of China's population live in the two municipalities of Beijing and Tianjin and the five provinces of Shandong, Hebei, Liaoning, Jilin and Heilongjiang. Most of these people reside on the fertile North China and Manchurian Plains.

Beijing has been China's principal capital since the 13th century. Today the Beijing-Tianjin conurbation is the largest in the country, with a combined population of about 16 million people.

The coastal province of Shandong has played an important role in the development of Chinese civilization since the earliest times. In the last century Shandong was beset by economic problems, resulting from natural disasters and overpopulation, and men from that province, together with foreign capital and technology, were subsequently responsible for opening up the virgin lands of Manchuria.

Beijing

With a grandeur and dignity few world capitals can match, Beijing is the political and cultural heart of China. The capital of the Mongol Yuan Dynasty, the Chinese Ming Dynasty, the Manchu Qing Dynasty and finally the socialist People's Republic, the city reflects the achievements of all these periods. Perhaps because of this Beijing is a city of paradoxes, a city with different moods, a city currently undergoing a transformation.

Early History The story of Beijing starts on Dragon Bone Hill, near the town of Zhoukoudian, about 30 miles from Beijing. It was here that a skull of an early ape-man *Homo erectus Pekinensis* , better known as Peking Man, was discovered in 1929. The skull dated back half a million years. In the same area skeletons were later found of cave men who also occupied the site some 18,000 years ago. Four thousand years ago there was a settlement near the present-day Marco Polo Bridge. Over the years the settlement eventually developed into a frontier trading town.

When the Tang Empire, which had been based on the Wei and middle Yellow Rivers, fell in the 10th century, there was an upsurge of 'barbarian' activity in the northeast. Beijing assumed a new strategic significance. It became a secondary capital of the Liao Dynasty of the Khitan Mongols, then the central capital of the Jin Dynasty of the Jurchen tribes, and finally, after being destroyed in the 13th century, it became the capital of Khubilai, Great Khan of the Eastern Mongol Empire, in 1261. By the time the great Venetian explorer, Marco Polo, reached Beijing at the end of the century, Khanbaliq, the City of the Khan, was already one of the world's great metropolises.

Beihai Park Little now remains of Yuan Beijing. Khubilai established his palace on an island in the middle of a lake in what had originally been an imperial garden of the Jin rulers. This was intended to be the centre of his city. It is now known as Beihai Park.

The palace collapsed in an earthquake and was replaced by a white Tibetan dagoba in 1651. This dagoba was at one time the tallest building in the capital. In Beihai's Round Fort, which overlooks Zhongnanhai (the headquarters of the Chinese Communist Party and the State Council), under a beautiful Yuan Dynasty white-bark pine, it is still possible to see the black jade bowl four and a half feet in diameter and carved with sea monsters, which was made for Khubilai in 1265 and formerly kept in the Yuan palace.

Beihai Park, Beijing.

The Ming Dynasty When the Yuan Dynasty fell in 1368 the capital was first moved to Nanjing. Beijing became the power-base of one of the sons of the new Chinese emperor. In 1403 he successfully usurped power from his nephew, the second emperor, took the title of Yongle and re-established Beijing as the imperial capital.

The townscape of the Ming capital was a magnificent imperial conception. Created in the 15th century, there were four walled sections. The Imperial Palace was the focal point of the grand design, arranged in the centre along the north-south axis of the city. The great halls of the palace, with their bright yellow-tiled roofs, and built on white marble terraces, were the highest structures allowed in the almost flat city. Around the palace was the Imperial City containing various court and governmental buildings. This in turn was the centre of the much larger Inner City, with its main streets laid out according to a grid. The rectangular areas between these streets were intersected by a network of little narrow lanes called *hutong* , containing the grey-walled, grey-tiled domestic courtyards of the common people. To the south the Outer City was a similar urban area newly

Gate of Divine Pride, Imperial Palace, Beijing

developed in the 15th century, but more randomly laid out. The Outer City
was given its own wall in the 16th century.

Imperial altars were built outside the Inner City. The Temple of Heaven
was located in the Outer City, the Altar of the Sun was built to the east of
the Inner City, the Altar of the Earth to the north and the Altar of the Moon
to the west.

The Imperial Palace Between 1406 and 1420 100,000 artisans and
a million workmen were involved in the building of the Imperial Palace.
Twenty-four emperors of the Ming and Qing Dynasties subsequently lived in
the halls, pavilions and courtyards of what has been called in the west 'the
Forbidden City'. Only seldom did they emerge into the world beyond the
red walls of their 250 acre home.

The Beijing palace is the largest and most complete imperial complex
remaining in China. It is a supreme example of Ming architectural style. The
scale is monumental but never oppressive, the design symmetrical but not
repetitive. There is an extraordinary sense of balance between the buildings
and the open spaces they surround. The palace has been restored,
repainted and rebuilt many times since the time of the Emperor Yongle,
notably during the long reign of the great Qing emperor, Qianlong
(1736-1795); however, the basic designs of the third Ming emperor remain
and can still be seen.

The palace is divided into two main sections. In the front, to the south,
is the Outer Palace, dominated by three great halls formerly used for official
and public purposes. At the back, the northern section is the Inner Palace,
which contains three large halls complementing the great halls of the Outer
Palace as well as many smaller buildings on either side, once the actual
living quarters of the imperial family.

Many treasures have been stolen, looted or otherwise removed from
the palace since the 19th century, but what remains is still remarkable.
Many of the old palace buildings are now used as exhibition halls. Fine
Song, Ming and Qing paintings are displayed, also bronzes, porcelain,
clocks, and a spectacular collection of imperial jewellery, gold, silver and
precious stones including a five ton jade boulder called the Jade Hill. Some
of the most exciting archaeological discoveries made in China in recent
years are also on show to the public.

The Temple of Heaven Another masterpiece of Ming architecture,
the Temple of Heaven, is entirely distinct in style from the Imperial Palace.
Nevertheless the blue-tiled temple has the same perfection of form and
space.

It was built by the third emperor as the setting for important rituals
designed to perpetuate the rule of the Ming Dynasty. The emperor in China
was regarded as the Son of Heaven, responsible to the celestial power for
the success or failure of his government. In very extreme cases Heaven was

considered to have withdrawn the mandate, and a new dynasty would be founded, with a new Son of Heaven. The emperor performed two rituals each year, to inform Heaven of the details of government, and to gain the necessary celestial confidence. Much later it also became customary for the emperor to pray for good harvests.

Symbolizing heaven and earth, the enclosure of the temple is rounded at the north but square at the south. At the southern end is a triple-tiered white marble altar, which was first built in 1530, and rebuilt in 1749. Immediately beside it is the Imperial Vault of Heaven, originally built in the same year: a round building with a cone-shaped roof of blue tiles. At the end of a long raised walkway is the magnificent Hall of Prayer for Good Harvests. This echoes the style of the Imperial Vault, but is much larger with a triple-tiered blue-tiled roof. It was built in 1420 as the Hall of Great Sacrifices, then rebuilt in 1751 and 1889 and given its modern name. The structure is entirely of wood, the tall round building being supported by 28 huge wooden pillars. Many of the articles used at the ceremonies, including musical instruments, are displayed in the Hall of August Heaven.

The Ming Tombs The site of the Ming imperial necropolis was chosen by the Yongle Emperor. He died and was interred in the Chang Ling mausoleum in 1424. There are 12 other imperial tombs located around the valley, but the complex is suitably dominated by the main hall in front of the Chang Ling. The Hall of Sacrifice and Ancestral Favour was built in 1427. It is supported by 60 massive wooden pillars, and surmounted by a resplendent imperial yellow-glazed tiled roof.

The only tomb to have been excavated is the Ding Ling, the tomb of the Emperor Wanli (1573-1620). Deep underground there is an impressive vaulted marble palace. It was built in the 1580s, well before the emperor's death, and cost 8 million ounces of silver.

The Great Wall at Badaling China's traditional defensive line against the peoples of the north stretches approximately 3700 miles from the Gulf of Bohai (see Shanhaiguan, page 56) to the west of Gansu Province (see Jiayuguan, page 119). One of the true wonders of the world, it is reportedly the only man-made structure visible from space.

Originally built in small sections by individual feudal states in the 5th century BC, the wall was later linked together by General Meng Tian on the orders of China's first great emperor, Qin Shi Huangdi, at the end of the 3rd century BC when he unified the whole of China. It has been rebuilt and renovated many times since then.

During the Ming Dynasty the wall was made of earth and rubble, faced with stone, and surmounted with brick, a material which hadn't been used under previous dynasties. Three Ming period sections of the wall have been restored. Badaling, about 50 miles from Beijing, is the most accessible, and is also the best place to see the wall in its most typical aspect, snaking across the mountain ridges.

The Qing Dynasty The Ming Dynasty collapsed in 1644, with the last emperor committing suicide in the face of a peasant rebellion. The imperial prize was won unexpectedly by the newly emerged Manchu leaders of the northeast, who had been invited into Beijing to help quell the rebels.

The Manchu tribesmen gradually became more and more Chinese in their attempt to be equal to their imperial responsibility. They were timid and conservative in their approach to art and architecture. They scrupulously preserved, restored and imitated the imperial architecture of the Ming.

Gate of Supreme Harmony, Imperial Palace, Beijing

The only notable Qing period site remaining is the Summer Palace of the Dowager Empress Cixi, the last effective ruler of imperial China. The other summer palace gardens and halls, including the interesting western-style Yuanmingyuan, were unfortunately destroyed by Anglo-French troops in 1860 and never rebuilt.

The Summer Palace The fourth Qing emperor, Qianlong, landscaped and embellished a summer palace called the Garden of Clear Ripples on the occasion of his mother's 60th birthday in 1750. Longevity Hill, the main landmark, was named in her honour, and the Kunming Lake was landscaped to resemble the West Lake at Hangzhou. The 18th-century palace was destroyed in 1860, but the Dowager Empress Cixi rebuilt it in 1888. Money intended for the building of a modern navy was used on the pretext that the shallow lake was suitable for naval training! The Dowager Empress called her summer palace the Garden where Peace is Cultivated. She restored it yet again, in 1903, after the buildings had been damaged during the Boxer rebellion.

Despite the decadence of some of the turn-of-the-century architecture, the Summer Palace is a delightful, rambling park full of curiosities, not to say follies. Three-quarters of the area is covered with water. Nowadays the lake is popular for boating in the summer, and skating in the winter.

The People's Republic After the Qing Dynasty fell in the 1911 Revolution, Beijing remained as the rather ineffectual capital of China until 1928, when the Nationalists replaced it with Nanjing. Beijing's status as China's capital was restored once more when Mao Zedong proclaimed the establishment of the People's Republic of China from the rostrum of the Gate of Heavenly Peace (Tiananmen) on 1st October 1949.

Beijing saw major changes during the three decades after 1949, as the imperial capital was transformed into the people's capital. The Imperial Palace, once the living centre of the city, became a museum. A new transport system around the palace became necessary as the original layout obstructed east-west traffic. To the horror of conservationists, both Chinese and foreign, the huge walls of Beijing and their great gates were progressively demolished. Few now remain. The decorative wooden arches called *pailou* were also removed, although there are still many of them to be seen in the parks. The new wide avenues which have been built have nevertheless been inadequate for the volume of Beijing's traffic. The streets today are choked with factory lorries, government and army cars, and the 3.17 million bicycles of the 9 million people of the capital.

Large new public buildings have made their appearance in the past 30 years, notably around Tiananmen Square. Museums, ministries and other pieces of architecture, to a greater or lesser extent either Stalinist or traditional Chinese in tone, have been put up: large, bare structures, they are more appropriate to the scale than to the sophistication of Beijing. Large modern housing blocks complement the official buildings. These blocks of long rectangular buildings with a dozen or more storeys are increasingly replacing the urban villages built along the *hutong*.

Despite these physical changes to their city, the people of Beijing seem to effortlessly retain their sense of style and manners. If the Shanghainese are bustling and businesslike, the people of the capital are gracious, relaxed and dignified.

Tiananmen Square The Gate of Heavenly Peace (Tiananmen) is part of the national emblem of the People's Republic of China, and the enormous square facing it can also be regarded as a symbol of modern China. This is partly because of the central location of the square in Beijing and the importance of adjacent buildings, and partly because of political events that have taken place there.

The square is a modern creation; it did not exist in Qing times. It covers an area of 98 acres, and until the middle seventies the square was used for massive parades and rallies, involving up to a million participants. In the centre is the Memorial Hall of Chairman Mao, with his embalmed body on display, as well as the Monument to the People's Heroes, an obelisk in memory of all the revolutionary martyrs of the 19th and 20th centuries. On the northern side of the square is the Gate of Heavenly Peace. The double gate, known as the Front Gate, is on the southern side. To the east and west there are the Great Hall of the People, the home of the People's Congress, and the two museums of Chinese History and the Chinese Revolution.

Tianjin

The municipality of Tianjin — more commonly known by its treaty port name of Tientsin — is famous for three things: superb, hand-woven carpets, tasty dumplings filled with a paste known as *gou bu li*, which literally means 'even dogs wouldn't touch them' and its quick-witted mercantile inhabitants who speak their own rich colloquial form of Mandarin.

Father and son.

The city itself offers none of the tourist attractions of other Chinese cities with longer historical traditions, but is a fascinating city to explore for its unique blend of rural and urban landscapes encompassing flat, dusty farmlands, vast orchards where the delicious Tianjin pears are grown, and modern post-revolution buildings which blend haphazardly with treaty port French rococo, Italian art-déco and British suburban-style architecture. Tianjin is not visually dull.

Visitors can enjoy leisurely strolls around the old city centre with its dilapidated temples and commemorative arches, and spend the evenings discovering the wide selection of restaurants which offer superb fresh seafood dishes. There is even an old Viennese coffee shop and restaurant known as Qishilin (formerly Kiesling's) which serves western-style food upstairs, and downstairs offers iced coffees and butter biscuits amidst marble, mirrors and potted plants!

The city is now no longer a bustling port, as the muddy Hai River which wends its way through the centre of the city has silted up and the modern port at Tanggu is now 30 miles downstream. However, Tianjin is one of China's largest commercial and industrial centres, and visitors would be well advised to visit the fascinating carpet factories, workshops for the carving of precious stones and the printing presses producing the famous new year posters which adorn every Chinese household over the spring festival period. Tianjin is also a centre for the production of terracotta figurines and a visit to the factory would afford a good opportunity of purchasing an attractive memento of the city.

The city boasts many good and comfortable hotels, several of which were built in the treaty port days, and an excellent museum of art which has an abundance of fine Ming and Qing paintings. Also of special interest is the Friendship Club which dates from the thirties and was previously the English Country Club. The club features an oak-panelled billiards room, a ballroom, an indoor swimming pool and an excellent restaurant.

Shijiazhuang

Shijiazhuang, an important railway junction and Hebei's provincial capital, is a flat, wide city of spacious avenues on the North China Plain. Until the beginning of this century, it was merely a village of no strategic importance. With the building of the Beijing to Wuhan and Shijiazhuang to Taiyuan railway lines, Shijiazhuang has evolved into a major industrial centre. The city itself possesses few places of historical interest except a military cemetery which boasts a fine pair of Jin Dynasty (12th century) bronze lions.

However, on the outskirts of the nearby town of Zhengding, there is a Buddhist monastery called Longxing Si which is well worth visiting. The monastery was founded in the 6th century, though the present buildings date back to the 10th century. The monastery is a series of large courtyards and temples set amidst verdant fields and has its own temple garden which the monks used to cultivate. The highlight of a visit to Longxing Si is the 10th-century, 71-foot high bronze statue of Guanyin, the Goddess of Mercy, which has 42 arms and thus reflects a period of Buddhist sculpture when the influence of the Indian artistic heritage still dominated the development of Chinese Buddhist art.

Chengde

Chengde lies 220 miles northeast of Beijing and is the site of Jehol, or Warm River, the beautiful 18th-century resort of the Manchu emperors of the Qing Dynasty. From 1681 the emperors used to escape the scorching Beijing summer and travel north, over the Great Wall, to the cool hunting grounds of Jehol.

Xumi Fushou Temple, Chengde

The wooded river basin in which Chengde lies is surrounded by pleated hills, punctuated at intervals by strange rock formations. The Kangxi Emperor created the palace, lakes and parks to blend in with the natural beauty of the site. The palace itself is an appropriately simple building, constructed of *nanmu*, a hard aromatic wood. The audience chamber, the Modest and Responsible Hall, is connected to the other chambers by *lang*, or covered walkways, that wind around the courtyards which are themselves shaded by ancient pines.

Through the palace it is only a few minutes' walk to the park and lakes. The Kangxi Emperor decreed that 36 beauty spots were to be created in the park. His grandson, the Qianlong Emperor, then doubled the number. As the visitor wanders beside the lake, there are carefully placed brightly coloured bridges which are designed to arouse his curiosity and lure him to one of the beauty spots — a pavilion such as the Hall of Mists and Rain, or the Golden Hill Pavilion.

Outside the palace grounds, the Qianlong Emperor built eight magnificient temples, seven of which still remain. The eighth which was built of bronze was removed by the Japanese during the war. The first to be built was Puning, or the Temple of Universal Peace, in 1775. This was a period in Chinese history of massive annexations, including Tibet and what is now Xinjiang Province. To integrate and, in some cases, to placate his new subjects, the emperor modelled the temples on their religion and culture. For this reason the Putuo Zongsheng Temple is a copy of the Potala at Lhasa in Tibet.

Beidaihe

Beidaihe on Bohai Gulf is a western-style seaside resort. Originally developed at the turn of the century as a summer refuge for foreign residents of Beijing and Tianjin, it now accommodates workers on holiday, recuperating patients, government and party officials, and day trippers, not to mention foreign tourists. A place to relax in rather than tour around, Beidaihe has 12 miles of fine beaches and a Austrian-founded bakery called Kiesling's famous for its ice-cream.

Shanhaiguan This is an ancient walled town guarding the eastern end of the Great Wall, only a few miles from where it meets the sea. Shanhaiguan is also located on the historical frontier between China and Manchuria. Its main landmark is a massive gate, built in 1639, with the bold inscription 'First Pass under Heaven'. A few miles to the east is a small temple commemorating a tragic folk heroine. Meng Jiangnü was the bride of a man conscripted by the first emperor of Qin to work on the wall. After many years of separation she went to look for him, only to find his bones embedded in the Great Wall. She committed suicide by jumping into the sea. The temple in her memory dates back to the 16th century.

Qinhuangdao The main city of the area lies between Beidaihe and Shanhaiguan. An important port, it is connected by railway to the provinces of the extreme northeast, to Beijing and Tianjin and to the nearby coal mining centre of Tangshan.

Jinan

The capital of the mountainous province of Shandong, Jinan lies at the foothills of the Li Mountains and three miles south of the loess-laden Yellow River. In the past, this river caused widespread damage in the lowlands of Shandong due to the innumerable shifts in its course. Jinan would prove worthwhile for those interested in archaeology as it is in an area of neolithic settlement sites. Fine specimens of black pottery have been found in the region. Today, Jinan is a thriving industrial and university city with many fine old German-style buildings which date from the beginning of the 20th century, when the Germans had effective control over Shandong as an economic zone.

The city has much to offer the visitor. It has various craft industries, excellent restaurants and its many springs, pools and lakes make it a Chinese Aix-en-Provence. The pools and springs are fringed with pavilions and teahouses which make for a relaxing afternoon of leisurely sightseeing. The outskirts of the city are girdled with mountains, many of which have been carved over the successive centuries. The most famous of these mountains is the 1000 Buddha Mountain which is now being restored after damage during the Cultural Revolution. Most of the carvings are Buddhist and date as far back as the Northern Wei Dynasty (6th century). The city also has a small museum dedicated to the 11th-century poetess, Li Qingzhao.

Sea and
Star Park,
Dalian

Tai Shan

All famous and scenic mountains in China have their share of temples and monasteries, and Tai Shan is no exception with its fine Daoist (Taoist) shrines and temples all dedicated to the Daoist deity — the Princess of the Coloured Clouds. The princess is a cult figure amongst the peasant women of Shandong — the province in which Tai Shan is situated — and even today the women, some with bound feet, still climb the mountain to pray for sons and grandsons, offering small gifts and coloured drapes to the princess. However, most modern sightseers enjoy the climb in the hope that they will glimpse the often elusive but magnificent sunrise when the sun appears like a ball of fire from a sea of clouds.

Tai Shan is the foremost of the five sacred mountains in China. Although it is only 4950 feet in height, Tai Shan was the mountain chosen by emperors as the site of imperial sacrifices to Heaven. The visitor must expect a strenuous climb up the precipitous paths and flights of stone steps which wind through pine-clad slopes. At the summit is the guesthouse and the main temple to the princess. At the foot of the mountain, the small town of Taian has a fine temple, Dai Miao, with an excellent fresco depicting an imperial progress.

Qufu A few hours away by train is Qufu, the birthplace of Confucius and the ancient capital of the state of Lu. Guests stay in the traditional courtyard complex which was originally occupied by the descendants of the sage. One can visit the Temple to Confucius and the Forest of Confucius, a vast forest burial ground for the descendants of Confucius. It is littered with their burial mounds and tomb guardians.

Qingdao

During the past 30 years Qingdao has developed into the main industrial city of Shandong Province, although it still retains the atmosphere of a seaside resort. Its attractions include a pier, an aquarium, and many fine beaches. It occupies a fine natural setting and enjoys a mild climate. The swimming season is from July to September.

Qingdao was originally built between 1898 and 1914 by the Germans, who selected the eastern entrance of Jiaozhou Bay, on the southern coast of the Shandong Peninsula, as a coaling station for their fleet. A modern city was built divided into the (European) residential, Chinese and business sections. Most of this can still be seen and is in a good state of preservation.

The other German legacy is the Qingdao (Tsingtao) Brewery, possibly the finest in Asia. The beer, which is exported, is made with water from Mount Lao, a nearby scenic spot.

Yantai

Better known in the west as Chefoo, Yantai is a fishing port on the northern coast of the Shandong Peninsula. It was opened to foreign trade in 1862 but never developed to the same extent as Qingdao. Industrial activity in Yantai concentrates on food and drink. Visitors can see the fish freezing factory on the jetty and the various orchards behind the town, as well as the Yantai Distillery which makes brandy. There is also a small but interesting museum, formerly a guildhall for merchants from the southern province of Fujian.

Early 20th-century German architecture, Qingdao

Shenyang

Shenyang is the main city of the extreme northeast, the area formerly known as Manchuria. It is a very important heavy industrial centre. About a quarter of all China's domestically produced machines are manufactured there, and it is also the hub of the region's communications system. Other nearby industrial cities such as Anshan (with the biggest iron and steel plant in China), Benxi and Fushun make the province of Liaoning, of which Shenyang is the capital, into the most industrialized and most urbanized in China. The industrial achievements of the province can be seen displayed in Shenyang's Soviet-style Liaoning Exhibition Hall.

Formerly called by its Manchu name of Mukden, Shenyang is also a historic city. After the unification of the Manchu tribes by Nurhachi (1559-1626), the great progenitor of the imperial line of the Qing Dynasty, Shenyang was made the Manchu capital. The Imperial Palace was built between 1625 and 1636, and became a secondary palace after Beijing became the main capital of the newly established Qing Dynasty in 1644. Although small by comparison, the Shenyang Palace is similar in style to the Imperial Palace in Beijing. It is also possible to visit the tombs of Nurhachi and his son and successor Abahai (1592-1643).

Lüda

Lüda is a double city composed of Lüshun and Dalian, located at the tip of the Liaodong Peninsula in Liaoning Province. Lüshun, formerly called Port Arthur, is a large naval base seldom visited by foreigners. Dalian, the principal port for the large industrial area to the north of it, is also a major manufacturing city in its own right.

Dalian is an exceptionally clean, spacious, well-organized city, much influenced by the Japanese and the Russians who occupied it during the early part of the century. It is also a seaside resort with four well landscaped beach parks. Its attractions include a large Museum of Natural History.

Changchun

The capital of Jilin Province lies north of Shenyang. It was developed as a capital for the puppet Japanese state of Manchuria between 1933 and 1945. It has some impressive administrative buildings, now mainly used by Jilin University. Changchun can lay claim to the title of China's Detroit, having one of the largest automotive industries in the whole country.

Harbin

Harbin, with its unique Russian atmosphere, is the capital of China's most northerly province, Heilongjiang. The city developed out of a fishing village on the Sungari River when the Tsarist government built a railway from Siberia to Vladivostok across Manchuria. A large Russian community remained in Harbin until the end of the last war. The old part of the city still has the cupolas and spires of some 30 Orthodox churches.

Harbin is intensely cold in the winter. People skate on the river, and the city holds an ice lantern festival together with exhibitions of ice sculpture, just after Chinese new year. The city now has an important and fast developing industrial area, producing amongst other things power-generating equipment.

The far Northeast is one of the most overlooked and least frequented areas in China. Severe weather conditions and underdevelopment of the tourist industry are probable reasons. There is much to be discovered here in the way of fascinating nature preserves, scenic sights and minority groups. You might even do some winter skiing or catch a very rare glimpse of the endangered Manchurian tiger.

THE YANGZI BASIN

The Yangzi Basin

If the great bend of the Yellow River is the cradle of Chinese civilization,then the Yangzi River Basin is the scene of its maturity. The area developed into an economically important region between the fall of the Han Dynasty and the reunification of the country under the Sui, who built the Grand Canal linking the lower Yangzi with the middle Yellow River.

The area flourished during the Southern Song, when the capital was at Hangzhou. The towns of Jiangsu and northern Zhejiang still have the atmosphere of the mellow, humanistic civilization of the Song. The expression of a soft climate and an easy way of life, the architecture of the towns is small in scale, never vulgar, never grandiose.

There is a well-known saying that is quoted in all China guidebooks — it first appeared in the west in Italian in 1612 — 'There is heaven above, and Suzhou and Hangzhou below'. Shanghai is another story...

Five Pavilion Bridge, Yangzhou

Shanghai

Shanghai, city of dreams and unkept promises, emerged from the sea just 5000 years ago. The city's name literally means 'up from the sea'.

Now one of the world's largest cities with a population of close to 11 million, Shanghai is China's largest urban centre. Shanghai started its illustrious career as a small trading centre to the south of the River Yangzi, on the left bank of the Huangpu (Whampoa) Creek. Shanghai played no role in the glorious days of the Chinese empire until the coming of the British opium fleet to Chinese waters in the 19th century. Shanghai was then jolted from being a quiet commercial backwater to becoming a thriving industrial metropolis. Shanghai's identity, even today, is still inextricably linked with those treaty port days.

The Treaty of Nanking in 1842 opened Shanghai, as a free port, to western trade and influence and, as a consequence, the city was quickly carved into spheres of influence demarcated by foreign concession areas, distinctly visible to this day. The old Chinese quarter of the city is to the southwest and skirts a curve in the Huangpu Creek. The international concession straddled the main thoroughfare, the immortal Nanjing Road, and the concession's eastern boundary was marked by the legendary waterfront known as the Bund. The French concession was in the southwest of the city and is still a distinct area with its stately tiled villas surrounded by lawns and high garden walls. Shanghai is still architecturally delightful and a stroll around the old concession areas or up the Bund can give a visitor a taste of how life must have been in the thirties or forties.

The Shanghainese themselves are a distinct group of Chinese people, who savour the differences between their lifestyle and that of the rest of China. They have their own mellifluous language which shows tendencies towards the polysyllabic, while their other Chinese brothers — no matter what the dialect — speak a distinctly monosyllabic language. The Shanghainese resist the central government's attempts to make them speak the universally accepted Mandarin dialect and retain their qualities of being more urbane, extrovert and daring than their northern counterparts. The Shanghainese also relish the form of Chinese opera, known as *Yue Ju*, from the adjacent province of Zhejiang, which has moved away from the more percussive northern opera styles, and features an orchestra with more string instruments and choruses sung in unison. Visitors would be well advised to treat themselves to an evening of this opera with its lyrical singing and romantic plots.

The most dramatic way of entering Shanghai is by river steamer and if that is not possible, you should take the four-hour boat trip to enjoy a skyline which resembles a shot of New York from a thirties film. The river is alive with all kinds of craft and as the main port of China, Shanghai and its river life offer a fascinating vista of the never-ending flow of ships loading and unloading. From time to time a junk in full sail can be seen to thread its way through the heavy river traffic and disappear up into the mouth of the Yangzi.

Shanghai is not only China's main port but is also the nation's major industrial centre, producing a wide variety of superb consumer goods which can all be purchased at the department stores in Nanjing Road or at the Friendship Store. Recommended items are the fine silk scarves, embroidered cottons and linens, woollen goods, warm silk jackets, cotton shoes, carved stone seals, traditional musical instruments, scroll paintings, brushes, painted fans and carved chopsticks. Department stores stock most major items but it is fun to explore the speciality shops and the little backstreet stalls in the old Chinese section of the city. Colourful stamps, comic books and posters also make ideal gifts. Visitors would also enjoy

The Bund, Shanghai

visiting the embroidery workshops and the precious stone carving factories, tours of which can be organized by the China International Travel Service representative.

Shanghai is a city which demands exploration, and visitors must not leave without visiting the old Chinese quarter with its narrow lanes, small stores and lively street life. In the northern sector of the quarter is the famous Yu Garden. It dates from the Ming Dynasty and although small, is a delightfully serene spot combining the grace of water, the wonder of stone and the beauty of plants. Paths meander through bamboo thickets and the visitor can delight in the sequence of small pavilions, pools, flowers and ornate gateways. One of the halls in the garden has been converted into a small museum detailing the history of the subversive Society of Little Swords, which planned an uprising against the Qing court in 1853 and used the hall as its headquarters. Adjacent to the Yu Garden is the Huxinting teahouse which perches in the centre of a small lake. It is an ideal spot for a rest and a refreshing bowl of tea.

Returning to the more modern areas of the city, an evening stroll along the Bund with its imposing European-style commercial buildings is a pleasure not to be missed. Trams shuttle past as young lovers stroll down a waterfront overshadowed by the large bank buildings which were once the scenes of hectic bustle as the Shanghai stockmarket rose and fell, fuelled by speculation, rumour, crisis and war.

Nanjing Road, the pulsating artery of Shanghai, invites exploration with its old hotels, various shops and restaurants and the unending stream of traffic and pedestrians. A quieter place for a walk is the area of plane tree-lined avenues of the old French concession around Jinjiang Hotel. People's Park is also a popular place — in the morning for calisthenic exercises and in the evening for family strolls. Nearby People's Square is an impressively vast open space which once saw some of the most violent rallies of the Cultural Revolution.

A favourite place for visitors is the Temple of the Jade Buddha, situated in the northwest of the city. The temple derives its name from its two fine milk-white jade Buddhas, one recumbent and the other seated on a lotus flower. The two Buddhas were brought to China from Burma in the 19th century and are still objects of great veneration. A few monks are still living and working within the temple complex, and a meal at their excellent vegetarian restaurant is a memorable experience. Longhua Pagoda is also worth a visit and dates back to the Song Dynasty. The eaves of its seven storeys are decked with temple bells which chime in the wind. The nearby halls date back only to the Qing Dynasty and contain a 10-foot high statue of the Amitabha Buddha.

Visitors to Shanghai also have the opportunity to visit various communes in the surrounding agricultural areas, or the famous Children's Palace which was once the family mansion of the famous and wealthy

Kadoorie family, who now live in Hong Kong. Also not to be missed are the Lu Xun Museum and Tomb. Lu Xun, one of the foremost Chinese writers of the 20th century, took up residence in Shanghai in 1927 and lived there until his death in 1936. He is most famous for his realistic short stories which satirised the social and political conditions of his time. Lu Xun's former residence can also be visited.

The Shanghai Museum of Art and History is rich in treasures and has a fine collection of rare bronzes from the Shang and Zhou Dynasties, when bronze casting techniques reached their apex and designs were based on primitive cosmological beliefs. The collection of ceramics and paintings spans the centuries. The dynasties best represented are the Song, Yuan, Ming and Qing. Shanghai is also a centre for modern artists, and visitors should not overlook the paintings representing the early 20th-century 'Shanghai School'.

Food is always an endless source of pleasure, and nowhere more so than in Shanghai. Some of the best specialities from other regions can be savoured in Shanghai, but don't miss the delicious Shanghainese dishes — steamed dumplings, freshwater shrimps and the famous Shanghai hairy crab which is available during the autumn months. Shanghai also retains its international flavour in its restaurants and the Red House Restaurant (Chez Louis before Liberation) is worth visiting as long as one remembers that the last French chef left the kitchens in the forties! The Deda Restaurant on Nanjing Road is an old German restaurant which still serves western dishes in the upstairs section, while the downstairs café is popular for its western-style cakes and lemon meringue pies. The old hotel restaurants also serve a hotchpotch menu of western and Chinese dishes, but it's more fun to explore the countless restaurants in the city whose old waiters have a surprising capacity to remember English.

Shanghai is effectively a very individual world of its own in contrast to other Chinese cities and the Shanghainese, rightly or wrongly, consider themselves a race apart. The city pulses with life and activity and has quickly adapted to new western influences. Girls sport permed hairstyles, young couples behave amorously in public and so-called fashionable clothes are worn with flair. Pictures of topless girls have been known to surface amongst the wares of street pedlars! As the main film-making centre of China, Shanghai abounds with cinemas. In the evening, crowds of young and old people jostle on the pavements for cinema tickets to buy a few hours of dreams. Streets are crowded, shops are stocked with an increasingly wider range of goods and advertisement hoardings glowingly describe products which cannot even be bought by the local populace. Shanghai has jumped a few decades into the eighties with a verve and style unparalleled in any other Chinese city. For sheer excitement and energy, Shanghai is a city *not* to be missed.

Spirit way, tomb of the first Ming emperor, Nanjing

Nanjing

Nanjing, meaning 'Southern Capital', is one of China's most attractive
cities with its broad and gracious tree-lined avenues and its relaxed and
vivacious inhabitants. Now the provincial capital of Jiangsu, Nanjing has a
history of over 2000 years and has been the capital of eight different
dynasties. In the 19th century, Nanjing became the capital of the rebel
Taiping Kingdom and suffered widespread devastation after the suppression
of the revolt by Qing and foreign troops.

Modern Nanjing is set in an agriculturally fertile plain and the River
Yangzi sweeps the northern edge of the city. The city would prove
fascinating for the visitor interested in ancient or modern Chinese history.

Nanjing was the capital of the Ming Dynasty and the old city walls
dating from that era can be seen in their now broken, but still massive,
splendour. The tomb of the founding emperor of the Ming Dynasty,
Hongwu, can still be visited although it suffered destruction under the
Taiping Rebellion and today only the stone gate, courtyard and tomb
guardians are still intact. The Linggu Monastery, near the Ming emperor's
tomb, also deserves a visit for its delightful setting in a pine forest. The
monastery is famed for its beautiful beds of peonies and other flowers.

The imposing Mausoleum of Sun Yat-sen is popular with resident and
overseas visitors alike, as is the Memorial Hall of the Chinese Communist
Party Delegation at Plum Tree Village where Zhou Enlai met with the
representatives of the Nationalists in 1946-7.

The city has an excellent history museum and in the centre of the city
is Xuanwu Lake with its islands, bridges, zoo and theatre. To the east of
the city are the Purple and Gold Mountains where one of China's major
astronomical research institutes is located. The famous Yangzi River Bridge,

Mausoleum
of Sun Yat-sen,
Nanjing

which was completed in 1968, is a spectacular feat in terms of post-1949 engineering, facilitating better rail and road transportation between Beijing and Shanghai.

Qixia mountain is a famous scenic spot, particularly in autumn when the maple-covered slopes are ablaze in their autumn colours. Qixia has three beautiful peaks. Set at the foot of the middle peak is the Flying Phoenix, the magnificent Qixia monastery which has a history spanning over 1500 years. The monastery's Buddha is carved from a single block of white marble, reputedly brought from Burma.

Nanjing is famous for its cuisine, hardly surprising in view of its imperial traditions. It is said that Beijing (Peking) duck originated in Nanjing! A lovely memento of the city would be a collection of Rainflower (Yuhua) pebbles which are bright, patterned quartz fragments and look beautiful when placed in water.

Yangzhou

The ancient city of Yangzhou was founded about four centuries before Christ and through the years it became renowned for its cuisine, beautiful women, arts and scholarship. Bordered by the Grand Canal but subsequently bypassed by the railways, it has lost much of its erstwhile importance. Today it has many interesting sights and crafts for tourists to enjoy. North of the city lies the Slender Lake spanned by the Five Pavilion Bridge, its yellow roofs perched on a triple-arched stone bridge. A copy of the Qianlong Emperor's barge ferries visitors around the lake. Opposite the temple on Flat Hill stands a serene Tang hall, Daxiong, and nearby is the Fifth Spring Under Heaven (fifth best for making tea!), so catalogued by Lu Yu, the Tang Dynasty tea expert.

Suzhou

Suzhou 'the garden city of China' was founded around 600 BC under King Helü of the Kingdom of Wu. In 1276 Marco Polo found it a bustling commercial centre. 'They live by trade and industry,' he noted, 'have silk in great quantity and make silken cloth for their clothing'. This prosperity was largely due to the Grand Canal, built in 605. It linked Luoyang, the then capital of China, with the area south of the Yangzi, including Suzhou and Hangzhou. Suzhou thus gained an important trade route to the north for its food and silken goods for which it was then, and remains today, justly famous.

It is to the scholar, on the other hand, that Suzhou owes its garden heritage. Colonies of literati chose this area because of its temperate climate and, if necessary, easy access to the northern capital. To be the kind of 'Renaissance Man' expected of him, a scholar required a conducive environment; for this purpose he would create a garden retreat. Today, although 11 large gardens, 27 medium sized and 69 small ones still remain, there are just six open to the public. They are a joy to visit: unlike the western garden they are not places of lawn and flowers, but of rock conglomerations, water reflecting intricate pavilions, and architectural tricks. Here scholars would think, paint, write poetry and debate with their colleagues. Perhaps the most exciting and indeed the smallest garden is that of the Master of the Fishing Nets, discovered down an alleyway in the centre of town. You enter through a nondescript door that gives no hint of what lies beyond.

Its gardens aside, Suzhou offers many other intriguing expeditions: a 53-arched stone Tang Dynasty bridge, a good museum, Tiger Hill, the supposed birth place of Suzhou's founder King Helü, and the Silk Embroidery Institute.

Perhaps most interesting of all is to wander Suzhou's narrow streets. Large bamboo poles laden with airing bedclothes hang from low whitewashed houses. Plane trees throw a dappled light on passers by. Stone bridges cross the numerous busy canals. You can listen to the local people conversing in their charming, slightly coy dialect. (It is even said to be pleasent listening to an argument in Suzhou). Spot the strikingly pretty young women, and try the delicious local specialities such as the steamed crabs.

Wuxi

According to legend Wuxi was founded by Prince Tai of the Zhou Dynasty some 3000 years ago. It gained its present name, meaning 'Without Tin', when the deposits were exhausted in the year 25. It is an old-fashioned city of water and mists, bisected by the Grand Canal which was built in 605.

One of the principal pleasures of Wuxi is to watch its bustling life from the elegant stone bridges that cross the smaller canals interlacing the city. Also the clay doll and silk filature factories are interesting to visit. To the west lies the vast Tai Lake, surrounded by fertile countryside as well as fine gardens and parks. A boat ride on the lake is well worthwhile.

Huang Shan

Towering to the height of nearly 6000 feet in southern Anhui Province, Huang Shan literally means ' Yellow Mountain' and if one considers that yellow is the Chinese imperial colour, one can easily understand the significance of such a name.

Huang Shan comprises 72 peaks, of which the most famous are: Lotus Flower Peak, Bright Summit and Heavenly Capital. The granite summits are accessible by walking trails, dotted with pavilions, temples and guesthouses. This area of scenic splendour is popular with Chinese

Huang Shan

holidaymakers and energetic tourists as the peaks and deep valleys offer
spectacular views over pine-clad slopes, strange and wonderful rock
formations and seas of clouds which often veil the higher summits. Streams
wind through the precipitous valleys and visitors can bathe in the famous
hot springs between the Purple Cloud Peak and the Peach Blossom Peak.

Hangzhou

The capital of Zhejiang Province has a setting of almost magical beauty.
It lies between the Qiantang River and the West Lake in a misty green
landscape of rolling hills and trickling streams. Hangzhou possesses a casual
elegance altogether different from the prevailing atmosphere of other great
historic Chinese cities such as Xi'an or Beijing. Long famous in China for its
scenery, the city has attracted many poets and painters. Two of China's
best-loved poets, Bai Juyi of the Tang and Su Dongpo of the Northern
Song, were governors there.

Hangzhou has been China's premier resort since at least the 17th and
18th centuries, when it was popularized by the Qing emperors Kangxi and
Qianlong. Descriptive monographs, virtual tourist guides, were published
from the 16th century onwards, together with woodblock prints of the
famous views of the area known as the Ten Prospects of the West Lake.

Hangzhou is not one of the oldest cities of China. The area now
occupied by the city and the lake was a shallow bay in the estuary of the
Qiantang River until possibly as late as the 6th century. Early settlements
were on the surrounding hills. The bay was in fact silting up but the
exposed sandbanks had to be protected from the destructive force of the
Qiantang Bore, an extraordinary tidal wave which still races up the estuary
during the spring and autumn equinoxes.

Bargeman on the Grand Canal, Wuxi

When dykes and later a sea wall had been built, and after the Grand Canal reached Hangzhou in 610, a spectacular development began, culminating in Hangzhou's most brilliant period as the capital of the Southern Song Dynasty from 1138 to 1279. By the 13th century it was the largest and most prosperous city in the world, as witnessed by an incredulous Marco Polo at the end of the century. From the Ming onwards it lost most of its political and economic importance. It was devastated during the Taiping Rebellion in the middle of the 19th century and most of its fine architecture was lost. Today the West Lake has been recently dredged and a huge tree planting campaign has enhanced the natural beauty of the city's surroundings.

Pagoda of the Six Harmonies, Hangzhou

It is a delightful place in which to wander. There are dozens of attractions. Many of those in and around the West Lake can be reached on foot or by boat. The largest island in the lake is called Solitary Hill. This is linked to the town by a causeway, named after the poet Bai Juyi, and it contains the Zhejiang Provincial Museum and Library, the Xiling Seal Engraving Society (the most famous of its kind in China), Hangzhou's best known restaurant called Louwailou and a beautiful teahouse overlooking one of the West Lake's most famous views, Autumn Moon on the Still Lake. Another popular spot, the Island of Little Oceans, is really a lake within a lake, a perfect setting for the lotus and water lilies.

Most of the surrounding area is farmed by the West Lake People's Commune. Their most famous crop is the green tea called Dragon Well. Visitors often call in on one of the production brigades en route to one or other of Hangzhou's famous pagodas and temples. Of the former, the best known is the Pagoda of the Six Harmonies, a sturdy octagonal structure dating originally from 970. The finest temple is Lingyin Temple. Founded in

326, it is in a splendid wooded setting opposite a cliff face carved with Buddhist figures during the Yuan Dynasty. The main hall of the temple is an impressive, high triple-eaved building containing a large modern Buddha.

Hangzhou has been one of China's principal silk producers since the Tang. Together with the two neighbouring cities of Wuxing and Jiaxing it was known as 'the home of silk'. Today the Hangzhou Silk Printing and Dyeing Complex is the largest silk factory in China and is frequently visited by tourists.

Shaoxing

A fine old, canal-lined town, this is the birthplace of the most celebrated writer of modern China, Lu Xun (1881-1936). The Lu Xun Memorial Hall is a museum built around the house where he was born. There is also a museum for Qiu Jin, an interesting early female revolutionary who was captured by the imperial forces and executed in Hangzhou in 1907.

The Temple of Yu the Great and his tomb lie outside the city. Yu was the founder of the mythical pre-bronze age Xia Dynasty traditionally, but not historically, dated 2205-1766 BC. He was credited with draining off the flood waters of the North China Plain and dividing the country into nine provinces. He subsequently became the subject of a local cult.

Shaoxing is also known for its yellow wine, made from glutinous rice, the best of its kind in China.

Putuo Shan and Jiuhua Shan

The two scenic areas of Putuo Shan in Zhejiang Province and Jiuhua Shan (Nine Flowers Mountains) in Anhui Province are both excellent places to relax from the hectic tourist city circuit. They are both sacred Buddhist mountains and offer the experience of stepping into a living Chinese inkwash painting.

CENTRAL AND SOUTH CHINA

HUBEI
Wuhan ●
Jiujiang
Lu Shan ▲
Nanchang
Changsha ●
JIANGXI
Fuzhou ●
HUNAN
FUJIAN
Xiamen
GUANGDONG
Guangzhou ●
TAIWAN
Zhuhai ● Shenzhen
South China Sea
Hainan Island

Central and South China

The two coastal provinces of Fujian and Guangdong and the three inland provinces of Jiangxi, Hunan and Hubei comprise the main area of the densely populated region of central and south China. The five provinces all have subtropical climates with hot summers, heavy rainfall and mild winters. Guangdong is the exception with its southern coastal strip within the Tropic of Cancer.

All five provinces have extensive mountainous belts interspersed with fertile alluvial river valleys and broad plains which produce rich harvests of the area's main crop — rice. The region's subtropical climate allows a long growing period and in all the provinces, two main rice crops can be harvested every year. However, Fujian's mainly mountainous terrain limits the amount of land available for agricultural purposes and, although rice is grown in the narrow, coastal river valleys and on the terraced mountain slopes, the people of Fujian have traditionally depended on the sea and forestry for their livelihood. In the four other provinces, agriculture dominates the economy with the main crops, apart from rice, being tea, sugarcane, tobacco, cotton, sisal and fruit. The tropical belt of Guangdong Province and Hainan Island is the main source of coconut and coffee for the domestic Chinese market.

The five provinces were amongst the last to be absorbed into the mainstream of Chinese civilization which spread southwards from the Yellow River. Even today, the cultural dissimilarities between the north and the south are still marked, and although the peoples of Jiangxi, Hunan and Hubei have dialects which have been directly derived from the northern Mandarin dialect, the dialects of Fujian and Guangdong are quite distinct with their profusion of tones, dialect words and implosive consonants.

Jiangxi, Hunan and Hubei possess large areas of alluvial lowlands dissected by rivers and lakes. In fact Hunan and Hubei derive their names from Dongting Lake, one of the largest and most famous in China, Hunan meaning 'South of the Lake' and Hubei meaning 'North of the Lake". All these provinces have remote mountainous areas of scenic splendour, and the northern mountains of Hubei are the home of fabled apemen who are sometimes glimpsed by the local peasants.

Fujian and Guangdong have deeply indented coastlines with good natural harbours. Their shores have been the homes of countless Chinese who set off overseas to make their fortunes in southeast Asia, Europe and America. Both provinces have been the focal points of foreign trade since the arrival of Arab merchants in the waters of the South China Sea during the Tang Dynasty. Today, both provinces flourish on the recent boom in overseas trade, much of it brought into the provinces by the trading houses of those overseas Chinese whose forefathers once knew the rocky shores of Fujian and Guangdong as their home.

Traffic police

Guangzhou

Guangzhou, more popularly known in the west as Canton, is a lively tropical city set on the Pearl River Estuary. Its close proximity to Hong Kong, so that its inhabitants have frequent contact with their relatives over the border and watch Hong Kong television, means that the city often seems a poor relative of that bustling, prosperous colony.

The Cantonese are the most outward looking group of Chinese people. They have traditionally travelled overseas to settle, and traded throughout southeast Asia. At the end of the last century, it was the Cantonese who spearheaded the migration of Chinese to the United States. So for the foreign visitor to China, the Cantonese are not strangers. Often the stock image the visitor has of a Chinese is based on the Cantonese, slightly built with a lively and cheerful personality.

The Cantonese do indeed have their very individual and distinct characteristics. The Cantonese dialect is totally incomprehensible to their other Chinese brothers as it has more tones and more final consonants than the other dialects. Their cuisine is considered the most varied and sophisticated of all the Chinese regional schools. The Cantonese have also shown a remarkable tendency to ignore the dictates of the northern political capital. In 1900, when the Empress Dowager Cixi declared war on the foreign powers, the Guangzhou officials ignored the edict and carried on trading peacefully with their foreign counterparts!

Guangzhou's setting in the fertile alluvial delta of the Pearl River and its tropical climate ensure that its street markets always abound with a variety of vegetables, fruits and flowers. At Chinese new year, when the northern plains of China are still under a blanket of snow, the people of Guangzhou are decorating their homes with sprigs of cherry and peach blossom on which they hang twists of coloured paper and gifts of lucky money.

The origins of Guangzhou are based in legend. The story is that five celestial beings riding on five goats and bearing cereals arrived in Guangzhou to found the city. Even today, the city is still often referred to as Goat City! In the Tang Dynasty, Guangzhou had already developed into a thriving port with visiting Arab traders amongst its populace. The Huaisheng Mosque in Guangzhou dates from 627 and is considered to be China's oldest. Local tradition has it that the mosque was established by Mohammed's uncle on a visit to China.

With the arrival of the Portuguese traders in the 16th century and the establishment of Macao as a Portuguese enclave, Guangzhou began trading with the European nations directly. Until 1842, when the Treaty of Nanking was signed, Guangzhou was the only Chinese port open to European traders. The first great Chinese entrepreneurs were based in Guangzhou and they actively participated in the trade of Chinese silks, tea and porcelain in exchange for Indian opium.

The First Opium War was precipitated in Guangzhou in 1840 when the court commissioner, Lin Zexu, burnt all the British-held opium. The opening of China to the foreign powers after 1842 led to the relative decline of Guangzhou as the main trading port of China. But the city was settled by western traders and missionaries who continued to exert great influence over its life until 1949. For example in the 19th and early 20th centuries, local opera was influenced by western music. To this day, Cantonese opera orchestras are the only regional troupes to have such western instruments as the violin and even the saxophone.

Bicycle park, Shamian Island, Guangzhou.

Until 1949, Guangzhou was a dilapidated city with a sprinkling of elegant European-style mansions for rich local and foreign merchants. Guangzhou also had a waterfront infested with the fleets of boat-dwellers who made an uncertain living from fishing and peddling. Today, the city of over three million inhabitants is a sprawl of modern buildings, factories and backstreets of traditional wooden houses. The city flanks the northern bank of the Pearl River and the main thoroughfare is called Liberation Road. Visitors can happily stroll the streets in the evening and feast at the countless restaurants without any problems. The Cantonese are used to the presence of foreigners in their city and pay them little attention.

Shopping in Guangzhou is great fun and one can choose from a wide range of handicraft products, silks, papercuts, furs and locally made pottery. Shoppers for antiques will also enjoy Guangzhou for its fine selection of traditional scroll paintings and old porcelain.

Guangzhou played an active part in the Republican Revolution in 1911. The local merchants unanimously took up the Republican cause led by the Cantonese doctor, Sun Yat-sen. Sun Yat-sen's Memorial Hall is frequently on a visitor's itinerary. In the twenties, Mao and Zhou Enlai were

Guangzhou (Canton) autumn trade fair

actively promoting peasant education in Guangzhou and one can visit the National Peasant Movement Institute, a memorial to those years of revolutionary activity in Guangzhou.

For visitors intent on exploring the old atmosphere of the treaty port days, a walk on Shamian Island, once the foreign enclave and residential district, is an interesting experience. The old mansions with their spacious gardens still stand. Towards the city centre is the old Gothic-style Roman Catholic Cathedral which is now, once again, open to worshippers.

Guangzhou's traditional temples are numerous — the Cantonese are considered to be a more superstitious and religious group than any other Chinese. The Hualin Temple, the Temple of the Six Banyan Trees or the Guangxiao Monastery are all worth visiting, the Guangxiao Monastery being the oldest with a famous, hollow Buddha in which were found miniature statues of its pious donors.

Guangzhou has many beautiful parks with seasonal flower displays, but the visitor should not miss a trip out to the surrounding countryside as well, to see the White Cloud Mountain Park which affords excellent views over the Pearl River Estuary. The Seven Star Crags is also a popular spot for visitors with its caves and the rock formation which resembles the pattern of the Big Dipper constellation.

Perhaps the most popular visit for the foreign tourist is to Foshan which means 'Buddha Hill', a small hill famous as a pilgrimage site. The hill abounds with temples and pagodas full of Buddhist images and carvings. Foshan is also renowned for its ceramics industry which originated in the Song Dynasty. Pottery is still manufactured there and tourists are taken to the factory where they can buy figurines and flower vases.

For visitors interested in the history of Guangzhou and its development as a trading centre, a visit to the Museum of History is recommended. The museum is in the historical five-storey Zhenhai watchtower overlooking the city. Each of its five floors contains an exhibition room with a wealth of artifacts, old maps, pictures and old books.

Xiamen

Xiamen, or Amoy as it is known in the local dialect, nestles on the mountainous coast of Fujian opposite the straits of Formosa and at the mouth of the River Jiulong. The city is now a blend of the architecturally old and new and, to a great extent, still relies on its traditional industry: fishing. Surrounded by attractive hills, the city dates from the Ming Dynasty and was the pirate stronghold of Koxinga, the pro-Ming buccaneer who terrorized the Qing troops and drove out the Dutch from Formosa in 1662. The city now houses an excellent museum which chronicles the lives and times of those Overseas Chinese who later became known as the 'Straits Chinese'. There is also a university for returning Overseas Chinese.

Old man, Shamian Island, Guangzhou.

Fuzhou

A port of call for Marco Polo, Fuzhou in the 13th century was already a thriving commercial centre for the trade in tea, pearls, fish and fruits. Foreign merchants from the Middle East and Southeast Asia flocked to the Fujian coast to trade at the various ports and many of the merchants settled in Fuzhou, creating small communities of Moslems, Jews and Christians.

Today, Fuzhou, on the north bank of the Min river, is the provincial capital of Fujian and the local population speaks the distinctive Hokkien dialect. Because of their seafaring traditions, the Fujianese have traditionally worshipped Ma Tsu, goddess of the sea, and the temples are once again thronged by worshippers. The city is set in the midst of beautiful hills, the most famous of which is Drum Hill. Visitors to Fuzhou will still find old mosques to explore. Lacquerware items and honeyed dried fruits are recommended souvenirs.

Changsha

Changsha is a city with a split personality, for it encompasses a very modern area of bland post-revolution buildings and an amorphous spread of traditional low dwellings which fan out from the city centre and sprawl into the suburbs. It is a delightful city for a quiet stroll in the evening when families congregate in lanes outside their small houses, chat, eat and relax in the traditional bamboo chairs, only found in the south of China.

Changsha, meaning 'Long Sandbank', is the provincial capital of Hunan and is split by the River Xiang which has created a long sandbank in its centre, hence the name of the city. Situated on the island sandbank is the Juzi Zhou Tou Memorial Pavilion housing a stone tablet on which is engraved Chairman Mao's poem 'Changsha'. Hunan was Chairman Mao's home province and it was in Changsha that Mao went to school and became involved in student politics. A trip to Mao's nearby birthplace, Shaoshan, is recommended. The area is scenically delightful with its traditional houses, well-irrigated fields and towering mountains.

Changsha has a long history as an area of settlement — artifacts dating from the epoch of the Warring States, when the area was part of the Kingdom of Chu, have been found. However, it is for its archaeological treasures of the Han dynasty that Changsha is famed. The Provincial Museum has the fine collection of treasures unearthed from the Mawangdui tombs dated to the Western Han Dynasty and visitors can see early lacquerware items, fine silk paintings depicting cosmological scenes, pottery, bamboo books, maps and early musical instruments.

Especially recommended is a visit to Yuelu Hill, with its fine views and beautiful old Buddhist monastery.

Changsha is famous for its marionette and shadow puppet theatres and visitors can also try the various restaurants offering hot and spicy Hunanese food. The regional speciality is *chou doufu* — stinking beancurd!

Arhat, Guiyuan Temple, Wuhan

Wuhan

A port stop for the Yangzi River steamers and a major rail junction on the Guangzhou to Beijing line, Wuhan is in fact a composite name for three cities straddling the confluence of the Yangzi and Han Rivers.

Hankou, on the north bank of the Han River, is the most modern and commercial of the cities, with its boulevards and elegant colonial-style buildings. The old racecourse, the creation and haunt of the foreign community in the treaty port days, is now a park with a zoo and stadium.

Hanyang, on the south side of the river, has the air of a more traditional Chinese city with its closely woven maze of low houses. Overlooking the confluence of the two rivers is Tortoise Hill which affords an excellent view over the busy river scene and has a temple dedicated to Yu, the founder of the mythical Xia Dynasty, on its summit. Also in Hanyang is a lovely monastery with a famous collection of 500 disciples of Sakyamuni and a 1000-eyed, 1000-armed statue of the Buddha.

Wuchang, the city on the east bank of the Yangzi, was established during the Han Dynasty and evolved as a walled city built on an axis. The city walls no longer exist but the ridge running through the city, Snake Hill, still has its stupa of white stone dating from the Yuan Dynasty and an old stone terrace which was the site of the Yellow Crane Pavilion. On the southern slope of the hill is the former headquarters of the 1911 Revolution, which started in Wuhan, and after it had spread throughout China, toppled the Qing Dynasty.

To the east of Wuchang is the scenic area of the East Lake with its temples and pagodas that provide a pleasant setting for an afternoon of leisurely sightseeing. Also in the vicinity of the East Lake is Red Hill with two pagodas set on its wooded slopes. Visitors are also recommended to visit the Historical Museum of Hubei in Wuchang, with its wealth of artifacts spanning many dynasties and documents relating to the revolutionary history of the province.

Nanchang

The capital of Jiangxi Province is regarded as the birthplace of the communist People's Liberation Army, which won the civil war in the late 1940s and went on to become China's regular army. On 1st August 1927 Zhou Enlai, later to become prime minister, and Zhu De, later commander-in-chief of the revolutionary army, led an armed uprising in the city following a breakdown in relations between the Nationalist and Communist parties.

Jiangxi's best-known industry has long been porcelain. The Jiangxi Provincial Museum in Nanchang includes a large number of ceramics, and the Arts and Crafts Gallery of Jiangxi has a display of modern pieces, some of them from the famous porcelain town of Jingdezhen.

Jiujiang

Jiujiang is the port of land-locked Jiangxi Province. On the southern bank of the great Yangzi River, it traditionally handled trade in tea and porcelain. Its importance has now rather diminished with direct rail connections from Nanchang to Shanghai. Most visitors today are en route for nearby Lu Shan.

Lu Shan

Lu Shan is a cluster of peaks rising 4836 feet above sea level, overlooking Lake Poyang and the Yangzi River. The resort town of Guling situated amongst these mountains is an ideal refuge from the intense heat of the Yangzi Basin summer. The temperature at the 3600-foot town can be 18°F (10°C) cooler than in Jiujiang.

Guling, with its curious English-style villas, has a number of beauty spots. Perhaps the best known is the Cave of the Immortal, where the Daoist monk Lü Dongbin is said to have mastered the secret of everlasting life. The Botanical Garden is the only sub-alpine one of its kind of China. Visitors can also see the former residence of Generalissimo Chiang Kaishek.

Xingzi, which is on the other side of Lu Shan beside Lake Poyang, has a number of scenic attractions as well as hot springs. Hydrotherapy is available for a variety of ailments.

The central and especially the south of China offers endless possibilities of interesting travel destinations. The easy accessibility into Guangdong Province from Hong Kong has extensively opened the area, which is excellent for short excursions from the British Territory. There are now over 40 open cities and counties, ranging from the tropical paradise of **Hainan** in the South China Sea, Special Economic Zones such as **Shenzhen** and **Zhuhai**, to less frequented rural areas in the outer regions.

THE SOUTHWEST

SICHUAN

Yangzi Gorges

Chengdu ● Dazu

Emei Shan ▲

Chongqing

Lijiang
●

GUIZHOU

YUNNAN
●
Dali

Kunming
●

Guilin ●

GUANGXI ZHUANG
AUTONOMOUS
REGION

●
Nanning

XISHUANGBANNA

The Southwest

The green hills and mountains of southwest China offer some of the
finest scenery in the People's Republic. The region is relatively under-
populated and under-industrialized, with only one major population centre,
the Red Basin of Sichuan. As a frontier area, the southwest has a number
of hitherto unassimilated tribal peoples, now called national minorities. Most
of them are related ethnically to the Thais, Burmese or Tibetans.

The flora and fauna of southwest China is by far the richest in the
country. The giant panda of Sichuan is world famous. It is less well known
that many of the garden flowers in the west originated from this area,
discovered by botanist-explorers in the late 19th and early 20th centuries.

Nanning

The capital of the Guangxi Zhuang Autonomous Region is just south of
the Tropic of Cancer, very close to the Vietnam border. It did not become
significant until after 1949. It is now a light industrial centre, important both
politically and militarily.

Eleven national minorities live in the autonomous region. Twelve
million of them are Zhuang, China's largest minority, a people related to the
Thais. They are unusually well assimilated, especially around Nanning, and
are often difficult for westerners to distinguish from Chinese.

Never experiencing the extremes of ice or frost in the winter, Nanning
is hot and humid in the summer. Over 30 kinds of tropical fruit are grown;
much of it is later canned. Every year on the 5th day of the 5th month
dragon boat races are held. Sleek, highly decorated boats each with 24
paddlers race along the Yong River, through the city, to the
accompaniment of loud gongs.

Yiling Cave,
Nanning

Guilin

Chinese poets and painters have been fascinated by the *karst* scenery of Guilin since the Tang Dynasty. Han Yu, a Tang poet, wrote 'The river forms a green gauze belt, the mountains are like blue jade hairpins'. Much of the more fantastic, perpendicular of Chinese painting has been inspired by the river and limestone peak scenery of the Guilin area.

Karst landscape, near Guilin

The northeastern corner of the Guangxi Zhuang Autonomous Region was under the sea 300 million years ago. Forced up by the movement of the earth's crust, layers of limestone were weathered by wind and water into eccentric, disconnected shapes often of great beauty. Below, enormous caverns were formed, offering an alternative scenery as amazing as that above ground.

Travelling 50 miles by boat down the Li River from Guilin to Yangshuo provides an opportunity to see a breathtaking panorama of *karst* scenery. The river passes feathery bamboos lining the banks, cormorant fishermen in small boats, local people selling tropical fruits, and picturesque villages as well as the rocky crags and peaks.

The *karst* formations extend right into the town of Guilin. In the centre, Solitary Beauty Peak offers a sheer climb up 306 stone steps, past innumerable old stone inscriptions, to a superb view of the town and its surroundings. The peak is in the middle of the former palace of a nephew of the emperor in the 14th century. Fubo Hill is beside the river and on top of an interesting cave with Tang and Song Buddhist carvings.

Reed Flute Cave and Seven Star Cave are the largest underground attractions in Guilin, much visited on rainy days. Both are illuminated by a series of carefully placed coloured lights. The Chinese enjoy giving names to the stalactite and stalagmite clusters, pointing out imaginary associations.

Guilin is an ancient city, founded in the 3rd century BC when the
Emperor Qin Shi Huangdi built the nearby Ling Canal to link the waters of
the Xiang Jiang (which flows into the Yangzi) and the Tan Shui (which
flows into the Pearl River). The canal may still be seen, running through the
delightful market town of Xing'an.

Guilin is also known for its bizarre menus. Local restaurants serve
snake soup, turtle, masked civet (a kind of wild cat), bamboo rat and
pangolin (scaly anteater) which can be washed down with snake bile wine.

Near Yangshuo,
Guilin.

Kunming

The capital of Yunnan Province enjoys an exceptionally pleasant
climate. Though close to the tropics, it is 6215 feet above sea level. Called
the City of Perpetual Spring, it has throughout the year a profusion of
blossoms: cherry, camellia, magnolia, azalea, cassia, plum and many
others. The local people are also colourful. Yunnan contains about half of
China's 55 listed national minority peoples, and many of them visit
Kunming in their national costumes.

Although in a frontier area, Kunming has the atmosphere of a major
historic Chinese city. It dates back to the Han Dynasty and many of its
attractive temples were built during the Yuan, when it was visited by Marco
Polo. Peasant houses in the old villages around Kunming are larger and
more substantially built than in many other, more central parts of the
country.

Kunming is a short distance from the northern shores of Lake Dianchi,
the sixth largest freshwater lake in China, formed by a fault in the central
plateau of Yunnan. Beside the lake is the Western Garden, an English-style
country house (now a hotel) built by a former governor of Yunnan. From

there it is possible to take a boat ride on the lake. High above the Western Garden are the Western Hills. The Yuan period Huating and Taihua Temples, both with courtyards full of flowers, can be seen on the way to the Dragon Gate, a stone arch at the end of a path cut into the cliff face above the lake.

On the other side of Kunming is the Golden Temple on Phoenix Song Hill, built at the end of the Ming Dynasty. The main hall is made largely of bronze which was once gilded. The temple was used as a palace by the great general and kingmaker of the 17th century, Wu Sangui.

The Stone Forest Visitors to Kunming often spend a day seeing the strange *karst* limestone formations at the Stone Forest in the Lu'nan Yi Autonomous County, 75 miles from Yunnan's capital.

The stone 'trees' are quite different from anything to be seen in Guilin. Jagged stone columns stand up to 100 feet tall surrounded by trees and small lakes. 270 million years ago a thick limestone layer formed at the bottom of the sea. When this was thrust up to become land, rainwater seeped through the rock opening up the sharp fissures which can be seen today.

Close to the Stone Forest Lake is the Sani village of the Five Trees Production Brigade. The musical Sani people are part of the Yi minority. Their women wear decorated and embroidered blue and pink costumes.

Yi national minority mother and child

Xishuangbanna

China's tropical paradise, the Xishuangbanna Dai Autonomous Prefecture occupies a corner of Yunnan Province on the Burmese-Lao border. Ten national minorities live in the prefecture but the largest group are the Buddhist Dai, or Tai, related to the people of Thailand. Early in April each year they hold a Water Splashing Festival. Everybody splashes everyone else in honour of a legendary struggle against a fire demon.

Yuantong Temple, Kunming

The tropical forests of Xishuangbanna have an amazing profusion of flora and fauna. Sixty species of mammals and 400 kinds of birds live in an area of 9600 square miles. There are elephants, wild boar, black gibbons, slow loris monkeys, helmet crowned hornbills and many more. There is an interesting Tropical Plant Research Institute actually located in the jungle.

Dali and Lijiang

Dali and Lijiang, two small towns previously only known to individual travellers that happened upon them are both located in northwestern Yunnan Province. Dali, home of the Bai minority, lies along the shores of the high-altitude Lake Erhai. A snow-covered mountain range is the backdrop of this ancient capital of the Bai Kingdom. Lijiang farther north, home of the Naxi minority, a former matriarchal society, rests at the foot of the 17,067 feet high Jade Dragon Snow Mountain.

Chengdu

Set in the fertile plains of China's richest agricultural province of Sichuan, Chengdu is an ancient city. A minor town during the Warring States period, Chengdu rose to prominence during the time of the Three Kingdoms as the capital of the state of Shu. Even today, Sichuan is often referred to by the name of Shu. Chengdu retained its status through the years and is now the provincial capital of Sichuan.

The city was once one of the most beautiful in China, rivalling Beijing, with its own viceregal palace. During the Cultural Revolution the palace was destroyed, and much of Chengdu has now been redeveloped. However, the city still retains charm with its craft workshops, small street stalls, relaxed outdoor-seating teahouses and a sprawling area of traditional-style houses clustered around the river.

Sichuan is the home of spicy Chinese cooking and where else to try the chillied beancurd and sizzling crispy rice dishes but in Chengdu? The Sichuanese people themselves are as lively as their food, with their immense good humour and wily tongues. Their local opera reflects their character and *Chuan Ju* is renowned for its humorous plots and slapstick comedy. The operas often feature *dame* roles with old gentlemen playing vulgar old ladies. Easy to understand even if you don't speak the language!

There are many sights in and around Chengdu. The countryside is attractive with villages of thatched houses set behind bamboo thickets (for coolness in the summer heat), double-cropped fields and the glistening terraced paddies. To the south of the city is the Wu Hou Ci — a temple commemorating Zhuge Liang, the great military strategist of the state of Shu.

Outside the city is the Du Fu Caotang, the 'thatched hut' of the great Tang Dynasty poet Du Fu who came to live in Chengdu for four years. Du Fu wrote many fine poems commenting on the tragic social conditions

Giant Buddha, Leshan, Sichuan

of his time and is greatly revered as one of China's foremost scholar-poets. The original hut no longer exists, but the area has gradually developed into a complex of halls, pavilions, ponds and gardens with fine specimens of bamboo. River View Pavilion Park in the southeastern suburbs is a peaceful spot for an evening stroll and it also has a collection of various bamboos.

There are many possible interesting trips in the environs of Chengdu. Green City Mountain is a beautiful area of rolling hills dotted with monasteries, temples and pavilions. A visit to Leshan, the hometown of Guo Moruo, the famous modern poet and playwright, is also interesting as the largest Buddha in the world can be found there. It is carved into the cliff overlooking the River Min. Also near Chengdu is the Guan Xian Dam where visitors can see the plans and layout for the hydraulic control of the River Min, which irrigates the fertile lowlands around Chengdu. This water conservancy project was initiated in 250 BC by the scholar Li Bing.

Perhaps the most interesting trip of all is to Emei Shan (Moth Eyebrow Mountain), which requires at least an overnight stay in the mountains. Emei Shan is China's most beautiful Buddhist mountain with its fine collection of monasteries. These can all be visited if the traveller is prepared for some hard walking and nights spent in temple accommodation with no running water or electricity. The mountain is a site of pilgrimage on the old Buddhist trail to Tibet. The monks still live in the monasteries and offer hospitality and incense to visitors. On the far and inaccessible side of the mountain live panda bears which can never be seen, although one can often encounter hordes of cheeky apes who steal food right out of one's hands!

Dazu

Situated between Chongqing and Chengdu in Sichuan Province, Dazu is one of the few places in China where you can see beautifully preserved Buddhist depictive art. Its remote location has kept it safe from both the ravages of time and recent political upheavals.

Chongqing

Chongqing, or Chungking, has been immortalised as the Nationalist headquarters during the Japanese occupation of China. Once a town of steep lanes and houses balanced on stilts, the town sits on a rocky promontory at the confluence of the Yangzi and Jialing rivers. Now a modern city with broad streets, it is still visually spectacular when seen from the river steamer which links Sichuan Province with downstream towns.

The city has few places of architectural interest although the main hotel stands as a monument to Chinese 'confectionery' architecture! However, around the city are places of scenic beauty including the Beiwenquan and Nanwenquan Parks, both of which have attractive gardens and hot springs for bathing. Jinyun Shan, or Red Silk Mountain, is well worth visiting for its coolness during the summer heat, its splendid views, innumerable species of subtropical plants and the fine Jinyun tea which is grown in the area. There is also an old temple on the mountain with a history of over 1500 years, containing many fine artifacts.

For those interested in communist history, visits can be arranged to Red Crag Village, where the 8th Route Army delegation had its headquarters from 1938 to 1946, during the Anti-Japanese War. Also of interest is number 50 Zengjiayan, where the South China Bureau of the Chinese Communist Party Central Committee was based and where Zhou Enlai lived.

Visitors would be well advised to try the various small restaurants which serve excellent Sichuanese cuisine, the basic ingredient of which is the *fagara* or hot chilli pepper. The local ice-cream is recommended and helps to cool the mouth after lashings of spicy food!

Yangzi Gorges

For the foreign traveller, the River Yangzi conjures up images of the days of 'gunboat' diplomacy when foreign steam vessels threaded their way up and down the Yangzi through throngs of junks and sampans. For the Chinese, the Yangzi (Chang Jiang or Long River as it is known in Chinese), is a river of spectacular scenery linked with the memorable history and battles of the period of the Three Kingdoms.

Chongqing
above the Yangzi River

Sani national minority woman, Stone Forest, Yunnan

*Log raft,
Yangzi
Gorges*

Today, a river trip for the tourist starts at Chongqing on a modern river steamer which has several classes of accommodation, but which offers a twin cabin with shower facilities to the foreign traveller. The journey to Wuhan, where visitors disembark, takes three days downstream with one overnight stop at the small town of Wanxian in Sichuan, allowing the steamer to traverse the river rapids by daylight.

As the steamer moves downstream from Chongqing there is a spectacular view of the city perched on the high riverr cliffs. At Wanxian, travellers are allowed to disembark for an evening stroll and shopping at the local handicrafts emporium. On the second day, the steamer reaches the river gorges and the visitor can spend the day on deck watching the unfolding spectacle of the muddy river rapids become enveloped by the towering gorges.

There are three main gorges: the Qutang, the Wushan and the Xiling. Each of the gorges has its own strange rock formations and tales which the guide explains as it is passed. The Wushan Gorge, which literally means 'Sorceress Mountain Gorge', is an eerie place whose name was derived from the belief that enchantresses haunted its slopes. The gorges are now easily navigable and one can still see junks in full sail plying this main artery of China's river network. Gone are the days of coolie labourers bending their backs to pull vessels upstream against the strong current. As the gorges give way to the flat river plain of Hubei Province, the steamer drifts past agricultural alluvial lowlands and, on the third day, arrives at the river port of Wuhan.

The southwest of China is rapidly becoming one of the most popular areas in China. Magnificent scenery, excellent food and colourful minority groups attract an ever increasing stream of travellers.

THE GREAT BEND OF
THE YELLOW RIVER

Datong

Taiyuan

SHANXI

Yan'an

Anyang

Kaifeng

Hua Shan ▲

Luoyang

Xi'an ●

SHAANXI

HENAN

The Great Bend of the Yellow River

The Yellow River is 3395 miles long, second only in China to the Yangzi River. It cuts through the world's largest loess plateau, and has the highest silt content of any river recorded. It has been both the joy and the sorrow of the Chinese, alternately irrigating the fertile land and devastating it with appalling floods.

The focal point of the river is the great bend to the east where the tributary, the Wei, meets the Yellow River on the borders of the three provinces Shaanxi, Shanxi and Henan. For the first 2000 years of recorded history the capitals of China were either near the Yellow River in Henan, or close to the Wei River in southern Shaanxi.

Xi'an

Now a rather undistinguished city of wide, dusty avenues and regimented modern housing blocks, Xi'an was once one of the world's most splendid imperial capitals to which foreign merchants flocked to trade in silks, porcelain and precious stones.

The modern city of Xi'an, the capital of Shaanxi Province, is built over the site of Changan, the immortal capital of the Tang Dynasty. In fact, the capitals of 11 Chinese dynasties have been sited around this area on the fertile Guanzhong Plain near the River Wei. It was also the last major urban centre on the historic Silk Road from central Asia.

Xi'an was an area of neolithic settlement. One of China's best-preserved stone age sites can be found just a few miles west of the city at Banpo. A village has been excavated and roofed in, and vividly patterned pottery and various implements can be viewed in adjoining exhibition rooms.

The first emperor of China, Qin Shi Huangdi, made his capital near present-day Xi'an, but his fabled Shanglin Park and Afang Palace were razed to the ground by the forces of Liu Bang, the founder of the Han Dynasty. With the establishment of the Han Dynasty and the development of trade with the Roman Empire along the Silk Road, Xi'an evolved into a major trading centre attracting the merchants of central Asia.

It was in the Tang Dynasty that Xi'an, then named Changan, reached the height of its prosperity. The city was laid out on a geometrical pattern, subdivided into quarters and market areas. The quarters were all enclosed by their own walls, and at night the curfew drum would signal the closing of all the gates between the city districts. Excavations of the old market areas have uncovered not only old Chinese coins but also Arabian, Byzantine and Persian ones. It was during this period that a strong Moslem presence established itself in the city.

After the fall of the Tang, the city never regained its former splendours and was only notable in the Qing Dynasty for social ferment and uprisings

Big Goose Pagoda, Xi'an

amongst its Moslem inhabitants. During the Republican era, Xi'an once
more assumed political significance with the establishment of the communist
base area to the north at Yan'an. In the so-called Xi'an incident in 1936,
the Nationalist leader, Chiang Kai-shek, was kidnapped in his pyjamas by
rebellious generals intent on forcing him into an anti-Japanese alliance.

Xi'an is so rich in history that visitors can easily overlook the modern
qualities of the city. It is an agricultural centre alive with street markets. In
the summer, the dusty streets are lined with watermelon sellers and the little
side-streets have a fascinating array of small stalls. Visitors should not miss
the opera costume shops where superb embroidered robes and slippers can
be purchased.

Vairocana Buddha,
Longmen, Luoyang

Visitors may be taken out of the city to the hills in the northwest to visit
the tomb, called the Zhao Ling, of the second Tang emperor, Taizong. The
ascent is along a dusty 'spirit avenue' lined with guardian tomb figures.
Another fascinating visit is to the Mausoleum of Qin Shi Huangdi, whose
tomb, as yet, has not been excavated. To the east of the site excavations
have uncovered one of the most spectacular archaeological discoveries that
a visitor to China will ever see — a vast army of terracotta warriors and
horses standing in battle line. There are over 6000 of these life-sized figures,
all with individually moulded features, hairstyles and clothing.

Within the city, there is the fine Shaanxi Provincial Museum, which contains the famous Forest of Steles, stone tablets with historical inscriptions. Two of China's oldest brick structures are in Xi'an: the Big Goose Pagoda and the Little Goose Pagoda. The former dates from 652, and the latter from 707.

Visitors will find the impressive Ming Dynasty Bell Tower in the city centre, and to its west is the Drum Tower, marking the Moslem·district of Xi'an. Today, many Chinese followers of Islam still live there, and the beautiful Ming Dynasty mosque with its courtyards and fountains has been reopened to both worshippers and tourists. The Moslems are very friendly and often have Turkic rather than Chinese features.

Yan'an

This bleak town on the Yan River in northern Shaanxi was from 1936 to 1947 the headquarters of the communists led by Mao Zedong, Zhu De and Zhou Enlai. The 8th Route Army arrived in the area in 1935, following the heroic Long March from southern China. Yan'an is of great historical and political importance. Policies developed during those years are still being discussed in Beijing today.

Mao and his comrades lived in caves cut out of the loess cliffs. Some of these are now museums. The town's landmark is the Yan'an Pagoda which has come to be regarded as a symbol of the revolution itself.

Northern Wei Dynasty Sākyamuni Buddha, Yungang, Datong

Hua Shan

Hua Shan is one of the traditional five sacred mountains of China. It rises nearly 7000 feet above the confluence of three important rivers, the Luo, the Wei and the Yellow River. It was formerly worshipped by the Daoists (Taoists). Pilgrims, poets, painters and others used to come to see its magnificent scenery of sheer peaks and precipices, waterfalls, springs, and venerable pine trees, as well as slopes dotted with old Daoist temples and monasteries. Hua Shan is not an easy ascent; in front of one particularly steep path called the 'Monkey's Frown' are two words carved into the rock: 'Turn back!'.

Anyang

Anyang is of major importance to archaeologists. The remains of Yin, the last capital of the Shang Dynasty, were discovered in 1899 near the village of Xiaotun, just outside Anyang. Yin had been the capital from 1300 to 1027 BC.

Much was revealed about bronze age history and social conditions. A royal palace, royal tombs, workshops and houses were excavated. Evidence was found of human sacrifices, a part of the Shang burial rituals. Fine bronzes, pottery and jade were discovered. Oracle bones and tortoise shells inscribed with early forms of Chinese characters have provided a great deal of information for historians and archaeologists.

Anyang today is a small industrial city. The Anyang Steel Plant was established during the Great Leap Forward in 1958. It supplies steel to the Luoyang Number One Tractor Factory as well as other factories in Henan Province.

Luoyang

Luoyang's prominent role in China's history is only rivalled by that of Xi'an. Luoyang was the capital of nine dynasties between 1027 BC and 937. It was the chief capital of the Zhou from 770 to 205 BC and again the chief capital of the Eastern Han from 25 to 220, flourishing during those years.

During the Northern Wei, a minor dynasty that had its capital in Luoyang from 493 to 534, the first Buddhist caves at Longmen were cut. The town itself reportedly had 1367 Buddhist temples at that time. During the Sui and Tang the city prospered, figuring prominently in the literature of the period.

People's Liberation Army girls posing for a picture.

Luoyang declined after 937. By the 1920s it had only 20,000 inhabitants, compared with a million over a millenium earlier. Since 1949 it has become a heavy industrial base. The Luoyang Number One Tractor Factory, formerly called the East is Red Tractor Factory, is the best known of its kind in China. Bright red tractors come off the assembly line at a rate of one every ten minutes.

According to legend the Buddhist scriptures were brought to China from India on the back of a white horse. This is the origin of the name of Luoyang's major temple, the White Horse. Originally founded in the first century, it is believed to be the oldest Buddhist temple in China, though the present buildings date from much later.

Longmen Luoyang is perhaps not the best preserved of old Chinese cities but this is amply compensated for by its magnificent collection of Buddhist carvings at the cave temples of Longmen just south of the city.

When the Northern Wei moved their capital from Datong to Luoyang in 493 they chose the sandstone cliffs on either side of the Yi River as the site for a series of Buddhist temple grottoes. These are the successors of those at Yungang (see page 108). Carving continued for about 400 years; in total, 1352 caves were cut into the rock.

The monumental Fengxian Temple Cave represents the finest of Tang Buddhist sculpture. It was cut between 672 and 675. The central seated

Buddha, 56 feet high, is believed to be Vairocana, the supreme, universal, omnipresent Buddha. Beside him are two disciples of the historical Buddha, then two bodhisattvas, two heavenly guardians and two defenders of the Buddha. The latter are tremendously powerful pieces of sculpture.

Kaifeng

Once the imperial capital of the splendid Northern Song Dynasty, Kaifeng is now a relatively minor Chinese city, an agricultural centre for the wheat growing province of Henan. Although light industry has been encouraged to develop in Kaifeng since 1949, the city is still predominantly rural in atmosphere with its handicraft workshops, street markets and a population of just over 500,000 people.

Kaifeng is a historic city, having been the capital of seven dynasties and a centre of early Chinese civilization in the Yellow River region. Many fine Shang Dynasty bronzes have been excavated in the vicinity of Kaifeng. In this region early Chinese rulers contended for power before the unification of China by the Qin Dynasty in 221 BC. After the Jurchen nomads swept southwards and sacked Kaifeng in 1126, causing the Song court to flee southwards to Hangzhou, Kaifeng never regained its imperial splendour. The poets of the Southern Song Dynasty often lamented the loss of their northern capital in their poems and songs.

Today, visitors to Kaifeng can enjoy the remaining fragments of lost splendour by visiting the Old Music Terrace, now known as the Yuwangtai after the legendary Emperor Yu, who was said to have tamed the floods which covered China in mythical times. The Yuwangtai is now a beautiful park where famous poets are said to have once sat and recited their poems. The Xiangguo Si was the foremost monastery in China during the Northern Song Dynasty and was founded in the 6th century. The present buildings date from the Qing Dynasty, and the monastery contains a fine statue of Guanyin which exhibits features obviously influenced by the Hindu tradition of sculpting.

Also of interest is the Dragon Pavilion, marking the spot where the King of Zhou had his palace during the Ming Dynasty, and where examination halls were built for the imperial civil service candidates during the early Qing Dynasty. The Dragon Pavilion derives its name from the finely carved stone cube inside, which depicts dragons on its four sides. The pavilion itself is in a beautiful setting surrounded by lakes and gardens.

Taiyuan

The strategic city of Taiyuan, the capital of Shanxi Province, lies at the northern end of the Taiyuan Basin, in the centre of the mountainous Shanxi Plateau. Today it is a heavy industrial city with a prominent steel works, though for years its primary function was to guard the western

approach to the North China Plain. From the time the first city walls were
built in 497 BC down to 1949, when the communist forces captured the
city from the warlord Yan Xishan, it was the scene of unparalleled
turbulence.

A number of monuments remain, despite the number of armies that
have marched in and out of the city. The Chongshan Temple contains a
fine Ming period hall with three statues of bodhisattvas with 'a thousand
eyes and a thousand hands'. The temple has a precious collection of early
printed Buddhist scriptures. The Shanxi Provincial Museum is one of the
best in China. It has a fine collection housed in a series of attractive old
buildings.

Cold rolling
mill,
Taiyuan Iron
and Steel
Company

Jin Ancestral Temple One of China's largest and most beautiful
temple complexes is located 15 miles from Taiyuan in a wooded setting
around three springs which form the source of the Jin River, in the foothills
of Suspending Jar Hill.

It dates back to around the 5th century and was established to
commemorate Prince Shuyu of Tang, the founder of the local state in Jin in
the 11th century BC. The principal building is the Hall of the Sacred
Mother, who was in fact the mother of the Prince of Tang. It was built
originally between 1023 and 1031, and then rebuilt in 1102. It is one of the
best surviving examples of Song architecture. Approached by a unique form
of 'flying' bridge, the double-eaved building has a richly decorated facade.
Inside are 43 clay figures representing the Sacred Mother and her
attendants. These are contemporaneous with the hall, depicting in a series
of individual portraits the Song period ideal of feminine beauty.

Datong

The main town of northern Shanxi, Datong, was built close to the
Great Wall on the Mongolian frontier and functioned as a trading centre.
Today it is a well preserved town on the railway between Beijing and Inner
Mongolia. The narrow streets in the centre of Datong remind many people
of the capital. It is now in the middle of one of the largest coal mining areas
in China, and appropriately has one of the last steam locomotive factories
in the world.

The Nine Dragon Screen is one of the treasures of the town. It dates
from the Ming and is similar, but superior, to two others in Beijing. The
vigorous dragons are made of glazed tiles modeled in high relief. There is a
similar Three Dragon Screen at the Guanyin Temple.

There are also two monasteries, side by side, which were founded
during the Liao Dynasty, called the Upper and Lower Huayan. The main
hall of the Upper Monastery dates from 1140 and is the second largest
temple structure in China. Inside are five Ming period statues of Buddhas.

*Steam
locomotive
works,
Datong*

Yungang Ten miles outside Datong are 53 Buddhist cave temples
most of which were cut out of the rock between 460 and 493, when the
town was the capital of the Northern Wei Dynasty. They were made at the
suggestion of a monk called Tan Yao, who was involved with the carving of
the first five caves.

It is a much smaller site than Dunhuang or Longmen , but it contains
much fine Northern Wei sculpture, and is the earliest collection of Buddhist
stone figures in China.

The caves are dominated by a massive, 56-foot statue of the historical
Buddha, Sākyamuni, with massive shoulders to correspond with
descriptions of the Buddha in scriptures.

INNER MONGOLIA

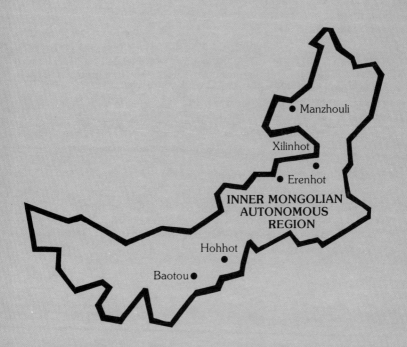

Manzhouli

Xilinhot

Erenhot

**INNER MONGOLIAN
AUTONOMOUS
REGION**

Hohhot

Baotou

Inner Mongolia

The Mongol people have haunted the imagination of the west as the
'terrible Tartars' whose 13th-century empire stretched from as far as the
Black Sea in the west to Beijing in the east. The ancestors of Genghis
Khan, Khubilai Khan and Tamburlaine, to name three of the most famous
Mongol Khans, were pastoral nomads whose homelands were the
unbounded steppelands of eastern central Asia. Today, with the imposition
of international borders on the people, they have found themselves living in
a divided land: Outer Mongolia is a Soviet sphere of influence and the
Inner Mongolian Autonomous Region is under the political control of the
People's Republic of China.

With the rise of Qing military power in the 18th century, the Mongolian
grasslands came under the influence of the court at Beijing. Until then, the
Mongol people had maintained their independence; sometimes coexisting
peacefully with their Chinese neighbours and sending tribute to the Chinese
imperial court and sometimes encroaching upon Chinese territory in search
of better grazing land and booty. The Chinese and Mongol peoples
traditionally maintained as uneasy truce and the Great Wall is a monument
to the fear in which the Chinese held their nomadic neighbours.

The Mongolian steppelands of eastern central Asia extend from the
Altai Mountains in the west to the Manchurian plateau in the east. The
Autonomous Region of Inner Mongolia was created in 1947 and is an
entirely political rather than geographical division of the Mongol homelands.

Inner Mongolia consists of 173,700 square miles of sparsely populated
plateau where the severe winters limit the development of arable
agriculture. It is estimated that of the population of 8.6 million people in
Inner Mongolia, only 20 percent are actually Mongolians, the rest being

*Young
musician.*

either Han Chinese or minority tribespeople. However, due to the climate of Inner Mongolia, the traditional economy of the Mongol people still dominates — the stockbreeding of sheep, cattle, camels and horses. Since 1947 there has been an increase of industrial activity in the region, much of it related to animal husbandry. The region is the main source of tanned hides, wool and dairy products for China.

The main crops of Inner Mongolia are wheat and potatoes, and the eastern forests also provide a valuable source of timber and paper pulp. A policy of afforestation has been implemented to protect the grasslands from the sand-carrying winds of the northwest. Industrial development is limited to the urban areas which benefit from Inner Mongolia's rich mineral reserves, particularly those of coal and iron.

Village beside the Ulan Bator to Beijing railway, Inner Mongolia

Although life in the urban areas of Inner Mongolia has been radically transformed in the 20th century, life in the grasslands remains very much the same for the modern Mongol as it was for his forefathers. During the warm summers, the Mongol nomads move their livestock across the grasslands to graze, living in houshold *yurts*. In the cold winter, where temperatures can drop to as much as -30°F (-34°C), the households gather in small communities for the winter months or move to the edges of towns where they are lodged in small housing complexes.

Summer heralds the traditional Mongolian festival held at Hohhot when the horsemen gather for races and competitions of equestrian skill. The Mongolian pony, so necessary to the livelihood of the nomadic people, is famed for its hardiness despite its small stature. In the 19th and early 20th centuries, foreigners living in China used the Mongolian pony for all their race meetings, and even interbred the ponies with English thoroughbreds to create the 'Z' class pony. During the week-long summer festival, visitors can also enjoy displays of traditional fighting as well as dancing.

Old man.

The Mongols as a people are a fusion of nomad tribes unified by Genghis Khan in the 13th century. They ruled China briefly in the 13th and 14th centuries in the name of the Yuan Dynasty. The Mongol conquest of China is generally attributed to their superior military tactics, derived from their greater stability in the saddle after the invention of the iron stirrup. Although during the Yuan Dynasty, marriage was discouraged between the Mongol people and the Chinese, many Mongols did assimilate themselves into Chinese society.

After the fall of the Yuan Dynasty, many Mongols returned to the grasslands and retained their separate lifestyle and language. Mongol is a phonetic language which is used to this day in Mongolia. The elegant vertical script of classical Mongol is still used in Inner Mongolia but in Outer Mongolia it has been supplanted by the Cyrillic alphabet. Temperamentally, the Mongol people are very different from their sedentary Chinese neighbours. Less reserved and cautious in their outlook on life, the Mongols are impulsive and magnificently hospitable people. A drinking session with a group of Mongol friends is an experience never forgotten!

Heroine of the Beijing Opera 'Lady Generals of the Yang Family'

Hohhot

Hohhot, a Mongol name pronounced *hu-hot*, is the capital of the Inner Mongolian Autonomous Region. Neither a very old town, nor a large one, it nevertheless has a number of things to see. In particular there is the grave mound of a great Chinese romantic heroine, the beautiful Wang Zhaojun, an overlooked concubine of a Han Dynasty emperor, who was forced to marry the chief of a Hun tribe in 33 BC.

Hohhot has many visitors who come to visit the grasslands on the other side of the Daqing Mountains, just north of the city. They travel to either

the Ulantoke or Wangfu Communes where they stay in *yurts*, the inner
Asian felt tent, and watch the herds of camels, horses, sheep and cattle.

*Wudangzhao,
near Baotou*

Baotou

Baotou is a more important industrial centre than Hohhot. It has a
large iron and steel works, as well as chemicals, textiles, cement and other
industries. The city was evidently planned on a grand scale after 1949, and
is very spread out. It is the largest city in Inner Mongolia.

An interesting Tibetan-style lamasery is located a few hours away from
Baotou. It is called Wudangzhao and was built during the 18th century. At
one time the lamasery owned 16,500 acres of land, 500 slaves and a coal
mine.

Manzhouli, Xilinhot and Erenhot

Manzhouli is best known as the entry point into China by travellers on
the Friday Trans-Siberian Express from Moscow to Peking. The Monday
express travels through Outer Mongolia passing on its way to Peking via
Hohhot. Xilinhot and Erenhot, both far removed from any beaten track, are
two of the surest places to catch a glimpse of Mongolian daily life.

THE NORTHWEST

The Northwest

The northwest is an arid region of deserts and mountains, appealing to the would-be explorer rather than the conventional tourist. In early times, merchants, officials and Buddhist monks travelled northwest from China, along a series of oasis towns and small kingdoms out to central Asia, the middle east and eventually the Mediterranean. This route became known as the Silk Road. The whole history of the northwest is closely bound up with the development of this trade route.

Starting in Xi'an, the Silk Road followed the Gansu corridor to Dunhuang, where it divided in two. One route went north of the Taklimakan Desert, the other south, the two joining again at Kashi (Kashgar) in the extreme west of the present-day People's Republic.

Today the northwest is of considerable economic importance. The railway has dramatically improved communications, and China's pressing need to exploit the region's rich mineral resources, including oil, has given it a high development priority. It shares a sensitive border with the Soviet Union, so that it is also of strategic significance.

The northwest is an area of great cultural diversity, offering the visitor the experience of meeting many of China's interesting national minorities. The Ningxia Hui Autonomous Region is seldom on tourist itineraries, though some foreigners cross through it taking the railway from Lanzhou to Inner Mongolia. It is the home of the Hui, Chinese followers of the Moslem religion. Numbering 6.49 million in total, they are widely scattered throughout China, and only a small percentage of them live in Ningxia. Many of them can also be found in Xi'an, Lanzhou and Ürümqi.

Gansu Province, historically the link between China and central Asia, is overwhelmingly Chinese though there are isolated communities of Tibetans and Bonan and Dongxiang Mongols in the south near Lanzhou, and Kazaks, Mongols and Yugurs in the north near Dunhuang and Jiayuguan.

The Xinjiang Uygur Autonomous Region occupies no less than one-sixth of the entire country. A large number of the inhabitants are now Chinese, the result of large scale immigration during the past 30 years. Nevertheless the various non-Chinese peoples who have lived for centuries in Xinjiang still exert a powerful influence on the cultural life of the area.

Most of the national minority peoples are Turkic language-speaking Moslems. The largest group are the 5.48 million Uygurs, a sedentary farming people who live in the oasis towns. Generous hosts who love singing and dancing, they are strikingly handsome with faces combining both Mongoloid and Indo-Iranian features.

Their ethnic cousins the Kazaks and Kirgiz are nomadic. Most of the Kazaks live in the mountains and their way of life is not dissimilar to that of the Mongols on the steppe. They are fine horsemen, keep sheep and goats, and live in yurts in the summer. The Kirgis keep herds of Bactrian camels.

The Xibe Manchus, living on the Soviet border, are descended from Qing Dynasty garrison troops and originally came from the northeast of China. The Tajiks on the border with Pakistan, Afghanistan and the most western part of the border with the Soviet Union are related to the Iranians. There are also Uzbeks, Tatars, Mongols, Daur Mongols and a few Russians.

Lanzhou

The burgeoning industrial capital of Gansu Province is the chief city of the northwest, at the centre of the whole rail system of west China, with connections to Xinjiang, Inner Mongolia, Qinghai and Shaanxi.

The long, thin city stretches from east to west along the banks of the Yellow River; most of it is new. The western end is industrial with a large petrochemical plant, an oil refinery (processing oil from the northwest), a machine tool factory and many others. Lanzhou exemplifies both the best and the worst aspects of contemporary Chinese industrialization. In the winter the city suffers from serious air pollution; it is also very cold.

Bingling Si Caves These Buddhist caves are in a site up the Yellow River from Lanzhou, which is only accessible during late summer. Bingling is the Chinese equivalent of a Tibetan phrase meaning '1000 Buddhas', a standard name for groups of Buddhist grottoes. The original name used

View of Lanzhou across the Yellow River from White Pagoda Hill

Maijishan

during the Tang was Supernatural Cliff Monastery. Some 36 caves and 80-odd niches were carved in the rock, the majority during the Tang, and some during the Northern Wei. The spectacular site is dominated by a large Tang Buddha.

Xiahe

Xiahe is situated high up in the mountains on the border region between Gansu and Qinghai Provinces, along the Daxia River, a tributary of the Yellow. It is the seat of the famous Labrang Monastery, one of the six most important monasteries of the Tibetan Yellow Hat Sect.

Maijishan

Maijishan means 'Corn Rick Mountain'. This rather strange shaped rock, with sheer cliff-faces and soft, easily excavated rock, was chosen, probably during the 5th century, as the location for a series of devotional Buddhist cave temples.

The caves, which date from the Northern Wei to the Song, contain clay figures and wall paintings. There are also stone sculptures evidently brought from elsewhere because the local rock is too soft for carving, as at Dunhuang. The caves comprise one of the four best collections of their kind in China.

Jiayuguan

The western end of the Ming period Great Wall is in Gansu Province, at a strategic spot on the ancient Silk Road, and close to the modern railway to the northwest. A large command-post was built at a place called Jiayuguan in 1372, on the orders of the first Ming emperor. It has been restored since 1949. There are two large gate-towers overlooking a panorama of desert and bare mountain, covered in winter with a coat of fine. wind-blown snow. (See also the Great Wall at Badaling page 50, and Shangaiguan page 56.)

Dunhuang

The 1000 Buddhas Caves of Dunhuang contain some of the world's finest Buddhist art. The oasis town of Dunhuang, known as the City of the Sands, was founded in 111 BC and became an important stop on the Silk Road. It was regarded by travellers as the first and last town of China.

Buddhism was introduced to China, via the Silk Road, in the 1st century, and the religion flourished in the international atmosphere of the frontier. The caves were begun in the 4th century and continued until the Yuan period. They were cut into cliffs some six miles from the town. Over 460 caves still remain, many of them in excellent condition due to the very dry climate.

The cave walls are decorated with highly detailed *tempera* paintings. The statues inside are made of painted clay as the sandstone rock was too soft to be carved. There are some marvellous examples of Tang sculpture.

At the turn of the century a library was discovered in a walled up cave, containing documents dating from around the 7th to 10th centuries. These are now mostly in London and Paris. Written in both Chinese and a number of central Asian languages, they have provided scholars with a wealth of information about Buddhism and central Asian history; there are also some unique examples of early Chinese vernacular literature.

Ürümqi

The capital of the Xinjiang Uygur Autonomous Region is right in the centre of Asia. It was never one of the main cities on the Silk Road, but the railway completed in 1963 has brought industrial development. It is now by far the most modern city in Xinjiang.

Ürümqi is a pleasant city with an interesting mixture of contemporary Chinese, early 20th-century Russian, and Islamic buildings, including a number of mosques. As the capital of the autonomous region it attracts many representatives of the national minority peoples as well as the indigenous Uygurs. Apart from the winter, which is rather cold, it enjoys a

Lake of Heaven, near Ürümqi

good climate in a valley between two mountain ranges of the Tianshan. On a clear day the snow-capped peaks can be seen from the city. There are no time zones in China: everyday life in Ürümqi just starts an hour or two later than in the rest of China.

The Lake of Heaven There is an extraordinarily beautiful alpine lake in the Tianshan Mountains, called the Lake of Heaven. It is 62 miles southeast of Ürümqi, below the glacier of Mount Bogda, at an altitude of

Kazak horseman, near Ürümqi

Crescent Moon Pool, Dunhuang

6400 feet. Surrounded by a ring of mountain peaks, there are forests of tall, thin dragon spruce above alpine meadows full of the scent of wild flowers. No greater contrast could be imagined with the deserts of Xinjiang.

Turpan

Lake Aydingkol in the centre of the Turpan Basin is 505 feet below sea level, the lowest spot in the world after the Dead Sea in Jordan. Turpan is by a long way the hottest place in the People's Republic, and has been nicknamed 'the Oven'. In the baked gravel desert outside the oasis the summertime temperature can sometimes rise to as high as 120°F (48°C). There is very little rainfall, as the water evaporates before it reaches the earth.

However, despite its extrordinary geography, Turpan has prospered for much of the past 2000 years. This has been due to the special irrigation system developed by the Uygurs. Surrounded by high, snow-capped mountains with fast running steams, the basin contains large reserves of water underground. The Uygurs have dug a large number of wells and brought the water to the oasis via underground channels called *karez*, in

Flaming Mountains, Turpan

order to prevent evaporation. With irrigation the area is one of the world's best places for growing fruit. Grapes and melons from Turpan are famous all over China.

Two ancient cities once flourished in the Turpan depression, important stops on the northern branch of the Silk Road. Gaochang, in the southeast, was founded in the 1st century. It was a square, walled city with a palace area and an inner and an outer city, modelled on the plan of an imperial Chinese metropolis. During the Tang it had a population of 50,000. It was abandoned in the 14th century for reasons still unknown, perhaps because of war, perhaps because of climatic changes. All that is left today are the brown crumbling walls and the foundations of buildings, but the overall city plan is still clear.

Some interesting finds have been made by archaeologists working in the nearby Astana cemetery. Tomb wall paintings and a variety of airfacts, and even corpses have been discovered in an excellent state of preservation, due to the exceptional climate.

The citadel of Jiaohe, some distance from Gaochang, was much smaller than the other city with an estimated population of only 6000. Its ruins are in

Tang Buddha, Bingling Si Caves

a romantic settings, perched on the top of cliffs, on an island between two small rivers. It was founded in the 2nd century and occupied until the 14th.

Turpan has been a centre for Buddhism and, more recently, Islam. The Imin Minaret and Mosque were built by the Uygurs in 1776. Entirely unglazed, the bricks of the minaret are arranged in bold geometric patterns. Inside there is a spiral staircase, winding around a central column.

The wall paintings of the 1000 Buddhas Caves, mostly of the Tang period, are now sadly mutilated, though they were once of comparable quality to those at Dunhuang. It is still an exciting sidetrip to the caves. They are in a magnificent setting in a gulch of the Flaming Mountains, a long row of red sandstone hills along the northern edge of the depression where the temperature can reportedly rise as high as 167°F (75°C).

Kashgar

Kashgar is the exotic oasis at the end of the Chinese section of the Silk Road, populated mainly by members of the Turgic speaking minority groups Uygur, Kazak and Kirgiz. Kashgar is a bustling, exciting oasis faithful to its name as a major trading city. The Sunday market takes over the entire city and is sure to rank as one of the most interesting and colourful markets in China.

TIBET AND QINGHAI

Tibet and Qinghai

Few places in the world are as mysterious as Tibet; few corners of the globe have been so effectively sealed off from the outside world. Throughout history Tibet has been physically difficult if not politically impossible to enter. It has been estimated that up to 1949 only about 1000 westerners were able to visit the Roof of the World. (The British military expedition led by Younghusband in 1904 accounted for about 600 of them.)

In the first half of this century the Tibetans lived in a medieval world dominated by religion and feudalism, the two being closely intertwined. The economy was undeveloped and hampered by the impossibility of proper communications.

The Tibet of the 1940s is well documented with photographs. Half the population were nomads, herding cattle, sheep and the indigenous Tibetan ox, the yak. They wore Tibetan robes, or *chuba*, made of sheepskin. They practised polyandry — one woman was often married to two or three brothers at the same time. Townspeople, much more sophisticated than the nomads, wore woollen cloth, as did the red-robed monks. The aristocrats wore silk brocade *chuba*. Aristocratic familes were often polygamous. Large amounts of jewelry were worn by all but the poorest members of society and the monks: amber, coral, and turquoise set in silver and gold, and charm boxes worn round the neck.

The staple diet was *tsampa* (a mixture of dried, roasted barley and yak butter), and yak meat. The only important imported foodstuff was Chinese tea. Sheep's wool was the main export, sent to British India.

The Tibetan world was considerably bigger than the present-day Xizang (Tibetan) Autonomous Region. It corresponded with the whole Qinghai-Tibetan plateau area, including the provinces of Amdo and Kham which were under much stronger Chinese influence than the Tibetan heartlands around Lhasa. Amdo today is administered as Qinghai Province. Kham is the western, mountainous part of Sichuan Province.

Tibet had been a protectorate of the Qing Empire in the 18th century but the Chinese had lost control of it by the beginning of the 20th century. The government of the People's Republic reasserted Chinese authority over Tibet in the 1950s. Following a rebellion in 1959 and the flight of the Tibetan leader, the 14th Dalai Lama, to India, Chinese policy in the region remained controversial. In 1980 the central government in Beijing announced new policies, aimed at winning over Tibetan opposition groups and accelerating economic development.

In the summer of 1980 wealth suddenly became the only qualification required of a potential visitor. Approximately 1000 western tourists became the first substantial group to see Lhasa since the British expedition of 1904.

Although many aspects of Tibetan life have drastically changed since 1949 — the nobility has left, almost all monastries have been destroyed —

Sera Monastery, Lhasa

much remains exactly as in old pictures. Ordinary towns-people and
nomads look almost identical in appearance to their parents and
grandparents — covered in jewellery, wearing heavy, ornate (and always
dirty) clothing. To what extent the economy has developed in the past 30
years remains unclear.

Tibet is still one of the world's great adventures.

Lhasa

Much of Tibet is so mountainous and so desolate that it is virtually

Mother and child,
Barkor Bazaar, Lhasa

uninhabitable. The historical centre of Tibetan civilization has always been
along the valley of the Yarlung Zangbo, 'Mother River' in Tibetan, which is
known as the Brahmaputra when it flows into India. Its tributary is the
Lhasa River. In this region in the southwest of Tibet, opposite the
Bhutanese border, are the three chief cities, Lhasa, Shigatse and Gyantse.

Recorded Tibetan history starts with King Songtsan Gambo (617-650)
who built the first Potala Palace in Lhasa, His successors ruled Tibet until
the mid 9th century. Thereafter Buddhist leaders took a prominent role in
government. In the 15th century Tsongkhapa, a reformist monk, founded a
new monastic order, the Gelugpa, or Yellow Cap sect. Subsequent leaders

Namgyal Courtyard of the Potala Palace, Lhasa

of this sect using the title Dalai Lama, 'Ocean of Wisdom', became both the spiritual and temporal rulers of Tibet.

The Potala, meaning 'Buddha's Mountain', became the winter palace of the Dalai Lamas. This triumph of Tibetan architecture, which can be seen today, was built in the 17th century by the fifth and sixth Dalai Lamas. It is a 13-storey structure built on a natural elevation in the centre of the Lhasa valley. There are two parts: the White Palace, built in 1653, and the contrasting Red Palace, completed in 1693.

The interior, richly decorated with murals depicting the fantastic images of tantric Buddhism, contains the living quarters of the Dalai Lama, ceremonial halls, prayer halls, libraries and bejewelled stupas containing the embalmed remains of previous Dalai Lamas. Below the palace buildings are the dungeons.

There are three important monastries in Lhasa. The Jokhang in the centre of the old city is the oldest, dating back to the 7th and 8th centuries. Sera and Drepung are both on the edge of the valley, and were built in the 15th century. The monasteries are all richly decorated, dark, mysterious buildings, full of the smell of yak butter which is burnt in devotional lamps. In each place it is possible to ascend to the flat roofs of the monastery and obtain magnificient views of the valley and the Potala.

Shigatse An increasing number of westerners are visiting this, the second city of Tibet and home of the Panchen Lama who ranks just below the Dalai Lama as leader of the Yellow Hat Sect. His monastery, the Tashilumpo, built in 1447, is one of the most beautiful remaining ensembles of Tibetan architecture.

Half the experience of going there is in the 11-hour land journey from Lhasa. There are two routes. One is over a 17,000 foot mountain pass below Xuegula Mountain, itself 24,600 feet high, and eventually crossing the Yarlong Tsangpo by ferry. The other is via the Kambala pass at 15,730 feet and the beautiful turquoise lake called Yamdrok Yumco, past **Gyantse**, the strategically situated third city of Tibet. Gyantse is the site of the magnificent Kumbum stupa which is said to be the finest example of Newari architecture in the world. Gyantse is also the site of the Dzong, a medieval fortress perched high atop a peak in the middle of the town from where the Tibetans tragically fought the Younghusband Expedition.

Other points of interest are the **Yarlong Valley** area, near Lhasa, especially **Tsetang**, seedbed of Tibetan civilization. Nearby is the Valley of the Kings, burial site of early Tibetan kings. In March 1985 the road was officially opened from Lhasa to the Nepalese border via **Xegar** (site of the Crystal Monastery), **Tingri** and **Zhangmu** (Kasa) at the border.

Qinghai is a vast province of windswept wilderness. The **Taer Monastery** near the provincial capital **Xining** was built in the 15th century and is one of the most important monasteries of the Yellow Hat Sect.

Tashi Lumpo Monastery, Xigazê

BIBLIOGRAPHY

Nagel's Encyclopedia-Guide China (Geneva 1978) is the established guidebook, but it was compiled in the 1960s and first published in French in 1967; it is now out of date. It has a wealth of historical and cultural information on the major cities, very much in the style of a traditional European guidebook.

China Guides Series have published *A Guide to Beijing, A Guide to Shanghai, A Guide to Canton, Guilin and Guandong, A Guide to Hangzhou and Zhejiang, A Guide to Nanjing, Suzhou and Wuxi, A Guide to Yunnan Province, A Guide to the Yangzi River, A Guide to Tibet and A Guide to Hong Kong.* These are a series of up-to-date, accurate and well-illustrated guides complete with the best available maps, diagrams and plans of cities, scenic spots and architectural complexes.

China. A Short Cultural History by C.P. Fitzgerald (Cresset Press, London 1961) is an excellent chronological introduction to Chinese civilization. An anthology, edited by R. Dawson, entitled *The Legacy of China* (Oxford University Press 1964) covers, section by section, the philosophy, literature, art, science, and politics of China. *East Asia: Tradition and Transformation* by J. K. Fairbank, E. O. Reischauer and A. M. Craig (George Allen & Unwin, London 1973) is a readable history textbook, and an excellent reference.

The Story of the Stone by Cao Xueqin, translated by David Hawkes (Penguin, Harmondsworth, volume 1 1973, volume 2 1977, volume 3 1980) is the great 18th-century novel of manners, better known as *The Dream of the Red Chamber*. This brilliant new translation will eventually be completed in five volumes, but the reader who wants to make a start on Chinese literature need look no further.

Chinese archaeology has attracted world attention in recent years. Two short studies explain the implications of the discoveries: *Ancient China: Art and Archaeology* by J. Rawson (British Museum Publications, London 1980) and *Ancient China: The Discoveries of post-Liberation Chinese Archaeology* by William Watson (BBC, London 1974).

The Art and Architecture of China by L. Sickman and A. Soper (Penguin, Harmondsworth 1968) is an absorbing introduction to its subject. *Style in the Arts of China* by William Watson (Penguin, Harmondsworth 1974) is an interesting handbook analysing the forms of Chinese art in terms of style. The great Swedish sinologue Osvald Sirén wrote a fascinating series of books on Chinese art and architecture: *The Chinese on the Art of Painting* (New York and Hong Kong 1963), *Chinese Painting, Leading Masters and Principles* (New York and London, 7 volumes 1956-8), *Gardens of China* (Ronald Press, New York 1949), *The Imperial Palaces of Peking* (London 1924) and *(The Walls and Gates of Peking* (London 1924).

Two other books on architecture can be recommended: A. Boyd's *Chinese Architecture and Town Planning* (Alec Tiranti, London 1962) and *Chinese Buddhist Monasteries: Their Plan and Function as a Setting for Buddhist Monastic Life* by J. Prip Møller (Hong Kong University Press, second edition 1967).

Chinese Monumental Art by P. C. Swann (Thames and Hudson, London 1963) covers a number of topics including the four principal Buddhist cave sites and the Great Wall. *The Nine Sacred Mountains of China* by M. A. Mullikin and A. M. Hotchkis (Vetch and Lee, Hong Kong 1973) describes the five Daoist peaks and the four Buddhist mountains.

Sven Hedin, the great Swedish explorer of the early 20th century, produced some very exciting material on Xinjiang and Tibet. He wrote *The Silk Road* (George Routledge & Sons, London 1938) and *Trans-Himalaya: Discoveries and Adventures in Tibet* (Macmillan, London 1909). *A Portrait of Lost Tibet* by R. Jones Tung is based on photographs taken in 1942-3 by Brooke Dolan and Ilya Tolstoy, grandson of Leo Tolstoy (Holt, Rinehart and Winston, New York 1980). A more recent pictorial study, *Tibet*, was written by David Bonavia and photographed by Magnus Bartlett. Published by Thames and Hudson in the U.K. and Commonwealth and by Vendome in the U.S.A. For those interested in both exploration and botany, *Plant Hunting in China* by E. H. M. Cox (London 1945) is recommended.

The Encyclopedia of China Today by F. M. Kaplan, J. M. Sobin and S. Anders (Eurasia/Macmillan, London 1979) has a lot of information about China's current economic and political set-up.

There are many books attempting to interpret the Chinese revolution. *Red Star Over China* by E. Snow (Gollancz, London 1938) is the classic report on the communists at the beginning of the anti-Japanese war, illuminated by the author-jounalist's long conversations with Mao Zedong. *Fanshen: A Documentary of Revolution in a Chinese Village* by W. Hinton (Vintage Books, New York 1966) describes in riveting detail the dynamics of revolution in peasant society.

Simon Leys is one of the most stimulating and penetrating observers of present-day China, concentrating on politics and cultural affairs. He has written *Chinese Shadows* (Penguin, Harmondsworth 1978) and *Broken Images* (Allison & Busby, London 1979).

INDEX OF
PEOPLE AND PLACES

Text by Simon Holledge (Beijing and 31 other destinations), Charis Dunn (Introduction:
The Chinese Kaleidoscope, Shanghai and 16 other destinations), Jill Hunt
(Visiting China), Harry Rolnick (Food in China) and Caroline Courtauld
(Chengde,Suzhou,Wuxi and Yangzhou)

Photographs by Magnus Bartlett (13,18,24,31,33,36,44,47,48,51,53,64,73,77,79,80,
89,90,104,105,112,127,128,129,131,143), Jacky Yip (23,26,29,34,43,110,117,118,
121,122,123,124), Simon Holledge (57,59,88,102,107,113,120) and Bob Davis
(111)/represented by Woodfin Camp and Associates, New York

Other photographs by Terry Duckham (55,91,92,94,97), Caroline Courtauld (62,67,68,72),
Herman Wong (96,98,101,103,108), Peter Kwan (5,71), Michael Holt (82),
Jill Hunt (114) and T.C. Lee (84)

Design and maps by Polygraphia Design and Production Limited

Printed in Hong Kong by South China Printing Co.

Lake Yamzho Yumco, near Lhasa